....

To

....

From

....

Date

GOD LISTENS

PRAYING *with* PASSION *and* POWER

by Jack Countryman

A Division of Thomas Nelson Publishers

THOMAS NELSON
Since 1798

NASHVILLE   DALLAS   MEXICO CITY   RIO DE JANEIRO

Published in Nashville, Tennessee, by Thomas Nelson®. Thomas Nelson is a trademark of Thomas Nelson, Inc.

Cover design by Koechel Peterson & Associates, Minneapolis, Minnesota.

Thomas Nelson, Inc., titles may be purchased in bulk for educational, business, fund-raising, or sales promotional use. For information, please e-mail SpecialMarkets@ ThomasNelson.com.

ISBN-13: 978-1-4003-2230-5

Printed in China

13 14 15 16 17 LEO 5 4 3 2 1

www.thomasnelson.com

"For I know the thoughts that I think toward you," says the LORD, "thoughts of peace and not of evil, to give you a future and a hope. . . . Then you will call upon Me and go and pray to Me, and I will listen to you. And you will seek Me and find Me, when you search for Me with all your heart."

JEREMIAH 29:11–13

CONTENTS

*Then those who feared the L*ORD *spoke to one*
   another,
   *And the L*ORD *listened and heard them;*
   So a book of remembrance was written
      before Him
   *For those who fear the L*ORD
   And who meditate on His name.
*"They shall be Mine," says the L*ORD *of hosts,*
   "On the day that I make them My jewels.
   And I will spare them
   As a man spares his own son who serves
      him."

MALACHI 3:16–17

GOD LISTENS

Wherever you are, whatever you're doing,
Every minute, day or night,
    ***I WILL LISTEN** when you speak to Me.*
Come to Me with a soft heart, a humbled heart,
An expectant heart, a heart alert for My voice.
    ***I WILL LISTEN** to everything you say.*
Speak to Me of your heart's desires, your dreams,
     your hopes;
Share your concerns and your fears.
    ***I WILL LISTEN**, for I have chosen you to walk*
     with Me,
And I will give you guidance and hope, peace and rest.
Remember to start each day with Me,
And remember that I walk beside you as the day unfolds.
    ***I WILL LISTEN** to you whenever you speak.*
Know that no concern of yours is too small for Me to
    care about,
And know that no mountain is too high for Me to help you
    climb—or for Me to remove.

I WILL LISTEN as you talk to Me
About both the little and the large in your life.
Keep in mind that nothing about you is hidden from Me;
You need not carry a load of guilt and regret.
  I WILL LISTEN when you confess,
And I will forgive you.
I will redeem the missteps and their consequences.
Open My Word and hear My voice.
Read My Word to reinforce your heart with My truth.
Meditate on My Word, and use them freely in your prayers.
  I WILL LISTEN for you to call.
I wait for you with open arms of love and care.
Never hesitate to start a conversation,
To pick up where we left off,
Or to simply tell Me "Thank You" or "I love You."
  I WILL LISTEN.

$\mathcal{I}$NTRODUCTION

$\mathcal{P}$rayer—the freedom to talk with the Almighty God, Creator and King, Shepherd and Father—is beyond question the greatest privilege bestowed upon the human soul. God invites us to turn to Him and talk to Him as we do with our closest human friend. This approach to prayer, however, can be very uncomfortable, if not very difficult, for many believers.

Communication with God is vital for our spiritual health and growth as well as for maintaining a strong walk with God. Furthermore, it has been said that each one of us stands tallest when we are on our knees. No wonder, then, that we often find ourselves sidetracked or distracted: the enemy works hard to introduce errors into our understanding of and commitment to a passionate and powerful prayer life.

Prayer is indeed the noblest activity of the human soul, and it also reveals much about an individual's spiritual condition. Are we spending time alone with God? And when we do, are we all there, ever present in the moment and focused on hearing His voice as well as sharing our heart? Or is prayer way too often merely a rote exercise, a mechanical playing out of what we know is good to do? May every one of us Christ-followers be so focused on God that communion with Him is natural, continuous, and life giving.

God longs for us to spend time with Him in prayer. He patiently waits for us to go to Him, and He listens attentively to our prayers. He blesses these times by lifting our eyes beyond our little world and selfish desires, by tuning our heart to the realities of His sovereignty, righteousness, and majesty. God also blesses our prayer time by conforming our desires and purposes to His will for His glory. No wonder prayer brings power and passion to our daily lives!

The Lord has also given His people—including you and me—prayer as a weapon for the spiritual war being waged 24/7. Prayer is to be our drawn sword as we battle against the power of darkness. We keep that sword sharp by continually communicating with God, and this ongoing conversation happens when we let everything we see and experience become a matter of prayer. This ongoing conversation also enables us to be more keenly aware of and more fully surrendered to our heavenly Father. When we are tempted, we can bring the temptation before God and ask for His help. When we experience something wonderful and good, we can thank God for blessing us with that gift. When all of life's circumstances and all of our thoughts and deeds become our opportunity to commune with our loving heavenly Father, we are leading a nourishing and God-glorifying life of prayer.

And the right attitude is essential for that kind of life. Our Father knows the thoughts we have in the privacy of our hearts without our even putting them into words. When He sees that He is the true focus of our prayers, we will receive a certain peace that only He can give. Our sincere and humble approach to our heavenly Father pleases Him.

One of the beautiful things about our gracious God is that He listens to us when we go to Him with an open heart, when we are sincerely seeking His will and direction for our lives. Many times in today's secular culture, we are easily drawn away from God. But when we stay close to God—we will live in His presence—when we talk with Him about every thought, event, question, feeling, and decision in our days. Prayer always draws us closer to our heavenly Father.

The holy Scripture is the spiritual food that nourishes and strengthens our relationship with God. When we choose to make Scripture a key element of our prayers, God's Word comes alive with relevance, significance, and truth. We receive the very breath of God as we communicate with our heavenly Father in prayer and through His Word.

This book is designed to help every believer have a more meaningful and more effective prayer life. As you read the prayers within this book, I want to encourage you to journal your own prayer thoughts to our precious Lord. The more time we spend in prayer, the more closely we will be walking with God. Prayer is, after all, a declaration of our dependence on God, our acknowledgment of both our neediness and His generous providence and care. Everything good in our lives is God's gift to us!

May these scriptural prayers draw you closer to your heavenly Father. Let His Word guide your conscience and shape your prayers of confession, thanksgiving, praise, supplication, and intercession.

The One who loves you with an everlasting love waits patiently for you to go to Him with a humble and repentant heart that yearns for a deeper relationship with Him. Beginning and ending and filling each day with an ongoing conversation with your heavenly Father will change your life.

Five Principles *for* Scriptural Prayer

1. What does God want me to *learn* from this passage? What truths is He teaching me?

2. What does God want me to *become* in light of these truths?

3. What does God want me to *do* in response to the lesson or the commandment found in this passage?

4. What promise does God want me to *trust* in?

5. What kind of prayer does this passage *prompt*?

A God-Given Priority

Be anxious for nothing, but in everything by prayer and
supplication, with thanksgiving, let your requests be made known
to God; and the peace of God, which surpasses all understanding,
will guard your hearts and minds through Christ Jesus.

PHILIPPIANS 4:6–7

Throughout His Word, God clearly makes prayer a top priority for His people. He gave us the prayer book of the Psalms, where we read this promise that David made to the Lord: "Evening and morning and at noon I will pray" (Psalm 55:17). God calls us to pray always (1 Thessalonians 5:17) and about everything (Philippians 4:6): whatever the challenge or trial, whatever the heartache or concern, believers are to make all our requests known to God. Jesus Himself modeled going off to pray early in the morning even when needy crowds clamored after Him. The Bible's commands and Jesus' example clearly communicate that prayer is to be a priority for us. A continuous dialogue with the Lord keeps us aware of His presence and open to His transforming work in our heart.

As God grows in us a heart for prayer and as we develop the practice of prayer, we also need to establish a place for prayer in our homes. Ideally, each of us will have a place of solitude free from distractions so that prayer can be private and uninterrupted. When we make prayer a priority like this—when we commit to practicing this demanding and rewarding spiritual discipline—we will grow spiritually, we will be more led by the Spirit, and we will be blessed by a richer relationship with our heavenly Father.

We tend to use prayer as a last resort, but God wants it to be our first line of defense. We pray when there's nothing else we can do, but God wants us to pray before we do anything at all.

Most of us would prefer, however, to spend our time doing something that will get immediate results. We don't want to wait for God to resolve matters in His good time because His idea of "good time" is seldom in sync with ours.

—Oswald Chambers[*]

[*]www.goodreads.com//author/show/41469.Oswald_Chambers, 23 May 2013.

CONFESSION

Confession—acknowledging our sins before our pure and holy God—is the path we take when we want to enter His presence. When we go before the Lord with a repentant heart, the Holy Spirit will show us those things in our lives that are displeasing to Him. Then, when we confess those sins and ask our heavenly Father's forgiveness, God hears our prayers, forgives our sins, and declares us completely cleansed of all unrighteousness. After all, that is His blessed promise to us in 1 John 1:9—"If we confess our sins, He is faithful and just to forgive us our sins and to cleanse us from all unrighteousness."

Instruments of His Righteousness

*Do not present your members as instruments of unrighteousness to sin,
but present yourselves to God as being alive from the dead, and your
members as instruments of righteousness to God. For sin shall not have
dominion over you, for you are not under law but under grace.*

Romans 6:13–14

Holy God, I confess that I am a sinner seeking Your forgiveness. I confess those things I have done that I ought not to have done. And I confess those things I didn't do but ought to have done. Cleanse me, O Lord, that I might know the sweet fragrance of Your mercy and the joy that only You can give. Then enable me, I pray, to not return to those sins You forgive. Break the power of sin so it no longer has dominion over me—and enable me to live, under grace, as an instrument of Your righteousness, in a way that pleases You and brings glory to Your name.

A Clean Heart

Create in me a clean heart, O God,
And renew a steadfast spirit within me.
Do not cast me away from Your presence,
And do not take Your Holy Spirit from me.
Restore to me the joy of Your salvation,
And uphold me by Your generous Spirit.

PSALM 51:10–12

Merciful and gracious Father, I have sinned, so I ask You to do what only You can do: "Create in me a clean heart." Lift me up out of the pit of my sinful ways and renew my spirit. I yearn to live in Your presence, refreshed and energized by the joy that comes with my knowing salvation in You. May Your Spirit guide my every thought, Lord, and uphold me so that I will walk in Your ways and wholeheartedly praise Your glorious name.

HEALING CONFESSION

Confess your trespasses to one another, and pray for one another, that you may be healed. The effective, fervent prayer of a righteous man avails much.

JAMES 5:16

Lord God, You call me to confess my trespasses to a brother or sister in Christ, to bring that darkness of my soul into the light. Give me, I ask, the courage to do so.

My emotions have caused me to speak hurtful words to those whom You love, and my guilt is ever before me. Place within my mouth the words that will be well received and bring comfort and forgiveness from those I have sinned against. Once You have declared me righteous and I can confidently enter Your presence, help me to stay in close fellowship with other believers in Christ. Guide my prayers for their everyday concerns, for whatever they may need, such as Your healing touch, Your comfort when broken, and Your everlasting love, so that they might experience a closer walk with You.

....

....

....

....

....

Cleanse Me!

Let us cleanse ourselves from all filthiness of the flesh and spirit, perfecting holiness in the fear of God.

2 Corinthians 7:1

Father God, I come before You as a humbled and needy child. Aware of how far short of Your standards I fall, I ask You to cleanse me from all filth and to wash away all the dirt of sin from my flesh and my spirit. Clothe me with Your holiness so that I will live righteously in Your presence. I know that holy and righteous living is not something I can do on my own, so, Holy Spirit, fill me with Your power that I might please my heavenly Father in all things.

PARDON MY INIQUITY

All the paths of the LORD are mercy and truth,
To such as keep His covenant and His testimonies.
For Your name's sake, O LORD,
Pardon my iniquity, for it is great.
Who is the man that fears the LORD?
Him shall He teach in the way He chooses.

PSALM 25:10–12

O Lord, Your paths are mercy and truth—yet I so easily and so often stray from them. I fail to obey Your commands, and, as You know, I like to be lord of my life. Forgive my great iniquity, my self-centeredness, self-absorption, and self-will. I do want to learn what You have to teach me about the ways You have chosen for Your people—for me—to live in this fallen world. Then may I show You my love, respect, and devotion by living according to the lessons You teach.

THANKSGIVING

F irst Chronicles 16:34 says, "Oh, give thanks to the LORD, for He is good!" Indeed He is, and we have much to be thankful for. We have a heavenly Father who loves us with an everlasting love. He patiently waits for us to go to Him with a repentant heart, confess our sins, and receive His gracious forgiveness and acceptance. Our expression of gratitude to God for all His blessings is a key component of our prayer lives. Giving thanks to the One who gave His only Son brings us into His presence, enabling us to know joy and hope in Him as well as His transforming touch.

A Joyful Shout

Oh come, let us sing to the LORD!
Let us shout joyfully to the Rock of our salvation.
Let us come before His presence with thanksgiving;
Let us shout joyfully to Him with psalms.
For the LORD is the great God,
And the great King above all gods.

PSALM 95:1–3

G reat God and great King, You invite me to enter Your presence with thanksgiving—but may I not stop there. After I consider with gratitude all Your gifts to me, may I tell others of Your greatness and Your blessings. May I shout joyfully of the salvation I have in Your Son. With all my heart, I thank You, who are "the great King above all gods," for the ways You lift me up, guide me, strengthen me, and bless me with peace. And, Lord, I ask You to give me a new song every morning—a song that celebrates the power of Your great love, a song that praises Your mercy that endures forever, a song that proclaims the truth that there is no one like You!

GIVE THANKS TO THE LORD

Oh, give thanks to the LORD, for He is good!
For His mercy endures forever.
Oh, give thanks to the God of gods!
For His mercy endures forever.
Oh, give thanks to the Lord of lords!
For His mercy endures forever.

PSALM 136:1–3

How thankful I am to be in Your family, Lord God! You *are* good—and I am humbled by and deeply grateful for the many blessings You shower upon me daily. Help me, merciful and gracious Father, to be the person You desire me to be, to stand strong against temptation, and to make my relationship with You my top priority. Cover me with Your presence and empower me to share boldly and with thanksgiving the joy of knowing You!

....

....

....

....

....

....

....

....

SET FREE FROM SIN

Do you not know that to whom you present yourselves slaves to obey, you are that one's slaves whom you obey, whether of sin leading to death, or of obedience leading to righteousness? But God be thanked that though you were slaves of sin, yet you obeyed from the heart that form of doctrine to which you were delivered. And having been set free from sin, you became slaves of righteousness.

ROMANS 6:16–18

Holy and compassionate Lord, I give thanks that Your Son, Jesus Christ, died for my sins and that I have "been set free from sin." Words cannot describe the depth of Your compassion for those who are lost, for those who are "slaves of sin." By Your mercy and grace, though, You have forgiven me. Now, I pray, teach me to be a slave of righteousness who lives every day in fellowship with You. Fill me with Your Spirit so that my life will be a testament to joy in Your presence and a beacon of Your light to those who are walking in darkness.

Joy in the Morning

Sing praise to the LORD, you saints of His,
And give thanks at the remembrance of His holy name.
For His anger is but for a moment,
His favor is for life;
Weeping may endure for a night,
But joy comes in the morning.

PSALM 30:4–5

Sometimes, Lord, I find it easy to sing praises and give thanks to You, the One who gives my life meaning. Yet other times my heart is heavy, and my weeping does "endure for a night." So I cling to Your promise: joy in You—joy beyond comparison, joy without end—will come in the morning, and Your favor "is for life."

Giving Thanks Forever

So we, Your people and sheep of Your pasture,
Will give You thanks forever;
We will show forth Your praise to all generations.

Psalm 79:13

As one of the "sheep of Your pasture," Shepherd God, I am blessed each day by Your protection, provision, guidance, and love. When I fall down, You pick me up. When I am weak, You are strong. May I "give You thanks forever" and boldly proclaim to future generations Your goodness, Your mercy, and Your grace.

....

....

....

....

....

....

....

....

....

....

THE LORD IS GOOD!

Oh, give thanks to the LORD, for He is good!
For His mercy endures forever.
Let the redeemed of the LORD say so,
Whom He has redeemed from the hand of the enemy.

PSALM 107:1–2

L ord God, You are good, and You are merciful. Through Your Son, Jesus Christ, and His sacrificial death on the cross, You called me to be in relationship with You, to even be called Your child. You redeemed me "from the hand of the enemy," from the eternal consequences of my sinful ways. Knowing that this redemption is rooted in Your unwavering mercy gives me peace for today, for tomorrow, forever. May I therefore always give You thanks, for You are good!

....

....

....

....

....

....

....

....

Thanks Without Ceasing

Rejoice always, pray without ceasing.

1 Thessalonians 5:16–17

Gracious and generous Lord, Your command is clear: "pray without ceasing"—and *without ceasing* means more than keeping a regular daily appointment with You. *Pray without ceasing* is a call to walk through life with You, to be open to Your guidance, to be aware of Your blessings, and to thank You for those blessings. So, I ask You, help me make thanksgiving an integral part of my prayers. And may my gratitude for Your goodness prompt me to "rejoice always"!

GOD'S GOOD WORK

I thank my God upon every remembrance of you, . . . being confident of this very thing, that He who has begun a good work in you will complete it until the day of Jesus Christ.

PHILIPPIANS 1:3, 6

Almighty God, just as Paul gave thanks in rememberance of the church at Philippi, I thank You for Your great faithfulness to Your people. As Paul did when he considered that body of believers, I also thank You for the "good work" Your Spirit has done in my life, enabling me to recognize both my need for a Savior and the truth that Jesus is the Savior. I thank You for growing my faith since that moment of salvation, and I thank You that You who have "begun a good work" in me will not stop until it is completed.

....

....

....

....

....

....

....

....

Praise the Lord!

   For it is good to sing praises to our God;

   For it is pleasant, and praise is beautiful.

Psalm 147:1

PRAISE

—⁓⁌·⁍⁀—

T hanking God for His many blessings and His gracious work in our lives is right and good; it is, in fact, a life-giving response to our heavenly Father. Also right and good is praising our Creator and Redeemer God for who He is, praising His infinite goodness and power, wisdom and love. God created us to worship Him, and He alone is worthy of our adoration and praise. So may the joyful cry of the psalmist be ours as well: "Praise the Lord! Praise the Lord, O my soul! While I live I will praise the Lord; I will sing praises to my God while I have my being" (Psalm 146:1–2).

When praise becomes part of our daily lives, our attitudes will change and the presence of God will be manifested in everything we do. It is a lifestyle that God will bless, and it will allow us to walk closer to our heavenly Father.

PRAISE THE LORD!

Praise the LORD!
Praise God in His sanctuary;
Praise Him in His mighty firmament!
Praise Him for His mighty acts;
Praise Him according to His excellent greatness! . . .
Let everything that has breath praise the LORD.
Praise the LORD!

PSALM 150:1–2, 6

Majestic, holy, and gracious Lord, You command me to praise You with my every breath—the breath You have given me. And I marvel, Lord, that You, who by Your breath created all things, value my words of praise and adoration. No matter where I am or what I am doing, I am to praise You—and I want to praise You. So I ask You, Lord, to give me a heart that will choose to praise You always and in every circumstance. Establish in my heart an attitude of praise for Your love and generosity, your mercy and grace, an attitude that overflows in words and songs of gratitude to You. Fill me with a spirit of joy that I might sing Your praises.

Praises Every Morning and Night

It is good to give thanks to the Lord,
And to sing praises to Your name, O Most High;
To declare Your lovingkindness in the morning,
And Your faithfulness every night.

Psalm 92:1–2

Holy and heavenly Father, You declare in Your Word that it is good for Your people to give thanks to You and to sing praises to Your holy name, to celebrate Your lovingkindness every morning and Your faithfulness every night. May I do exactly that as I walk with You and recognize Your presence in my life throughout each day. When I come to You with praise, I am truly blessed by Your mercy and grace. Enable me to live each day in the center of Your will so that I can serve You always with a grateful and joyful heart.

Living Praise

"I am the vine, you are the branches. He who abides in Me, and I in him, bears much fruit; for without Me you can do nothing. If anyone does not abide in Me, he is cast out as a branch and is withered; and they gather them and throw them into the fire, and they are burned. If you abide in Me, and My words abide in you, you will ask what you desire, and it shall be done for you."

JOHN 15:5–7

Lord Jesus, You clearly state that the only way I can play a significant role in Your kingdom—the only way I can bear "much fruit"—is by abiding in You and then allowing You to work through me. You have said, "Without Me you can do nothing," so teach me to abide in Your presence. And place within my heart a burning desire to seek You in all things. Then may I live out my praise to You by pleasing You in all I say and do.

....

....

....

....

....

....

....

God's Tender Mercies

The LORD is good to all,
And His tender mercies are over all His works.
All Your works shall praise You, O LORD,
And Your saints shall bless You.

PSALM 145:9–10

Gracious and merciful God, I know You want every part of me—body, soul, and spirit—and I do desire to grow close to You, to experience with You a relationship that is joyful beyond description. You who are "good to all" are indeed the Source of all my blessings. You are the great Provider who daily opens heaven's window and showers me with Your grace, mercy, and love. Each day Your "tender mercies" mean forgiveness for my shortcomings and sins, refreshment for my spirit, and guidance for my steps. How can I ever thank You enough? I will praise You daily and worship You with every part of my being. All praise to Your holy name!

OUR INCOMPARABLE GOD

Now to Him who is able to do exceedingly abundantly above all
that we ask or think, according to the power that works in us,
to Him be glory in the church by Christ Jesus to all generations,
forever and ever. Amen.

EPHESIANS 3:20–21

Indescribable and incomparable God, I know You love to bless Your people with answers to our prayers that far exceed anything we can imagine. I praise You for Your wonderful heart of generous love and for the infinite power of Your Spirit that works within us for Your glory and our benefit. Open my eyes each day to opportunities You give me to share with others the wonder of Your unlimited love, mercy, and grace. You alone, O Lord, are worthy to be praised, now and forever and ever!

An Upright Heart

I will praise You with uprightness of heart,
When I learn Your righteous judgments.
I will keep Your statutes.

Psalm 119:7–8

Pure and holy Lord, I come to You with a heart made upright only by Your grace. And blessed by Your grace, I will seek—in the power of Your Spirit—to "keep Your statutes," to obey You always. Do not let me wander, but hold me close. Teach me Your righteous judgments and help me hide Your Word in my heart so that I might not sin against You. Enable me to walk according to the truth of Your Word, keeping Your statutes and bringing honor to Your name.

Give ear to my words, O Lord,
Consider my meditation.
Give heed to the voice of my cry,
My King and my God,
For to You I will pray.
My voice You shall hear in the morning, O Lord;
In the morning I will direct it to You,
And I will look up. . . .
For You, O Lord, will bless the righteous;
With favor You will surround him as with
a shield.

Psalm 5:1–3, 12

SUPPLICATION

—❧··❧—

W hat a privilege to go before God and to humbly and earnestly share with Him our concerns and our requests! He actually invites us to pour our hearts out to Him, to share our requests and our needs. Our heavenly Father wants to be involved in every detail of our lives. Why? Simply and wonderfully because He loves us, and He delights in demonstrating His love by supplying our needs and thereby bringing glory to His name. His great love is the reason we can do with reverence and awe what God, through the writer of Hebrews, calls us to do: "Come boldly to the throne of grace, that we may obtain mercy and find grace to help in time of need" (Hebrews 4:16).

Remember He listens and cares for us beyond our imagination. Our requests and His listening ear are just a prayer away.

TEACH ME GOOD JUDGMENT

Teach me good judgment and knowledge,
For I believe Your commandments.
Before I was afflicted I went astray,
But now I keep Your word.
You are good, and do good;
Teach me Your statutes.

PSALM 119:66–68

I am all too aware, Lord God, that I easily go astray, that my decisions are not always in line with Your best for me, that I tend to do what I want to do. Because of my selfishness, I neglect to include You in my everyday life. I need You, Lord, to teach me good judgment, knowledge, and wisdom. I need You to help me "keep Your word." Place within my heart the desire to include You in all things. Give me a yearning to know Your Word that I may be blessed by Your wisdom. Teach me Your statutes so that I may witness to others and boldly share the wonder of Your great love. For You are all things good; You are worthy of my full devotion and praise.

LEAD ME, LORD

Thus says the LORD, your Redeemer,
The Holy One of Israel:
"I am the LORD your God,
Who teaches you to profit,
Who leads you by the way you should go."

ISAIAH 48:17

My Lord and my Redeemer, help me day and night to approach Your throne with an open heart that is receptive to Your voice. For I continually stray in my thoughts and actions; I go my own way and constantly stumble. I confess that I am lost without You and that I need Your Spirit to guide my steps moment by moment in all that I do. Be my Teacher, be my Guide, and show me "the way [I] should go." Teach me to profit as I entrust my life to You and live according to Your will. Bless me, Father, that I may bless others.

LORD, HEAR MY VOICE!

Lord, hear my voice!
Let Your ears be attentive
To the voice of my supplications.
If You, LORD, should mark iniquities,
O Lord, who could stand?
But there is forgiveness with You,
That You may be feared.
I wait for the LORD, my soul waits,
And in His word I do hope.

PSALM 130:2–5

Ever-present and all-knowing God, You know my needs better than I do, and You can meet those needs in a way far better than I would plan or request. So I find hope in You, the One who provides for my greatest need by forgiving my sin. If You, Lord, were to keep track of my sinful words and deeds and thoughts, I could not stand before You! "But there is forgiveness with You," and I am free to approach You as Your child. So as I cry out, "Lord, hear my voice!" I trust in You with all my heart, knowing that Your ways are far better than my own and Your thoughts much higher than mine.

LORD, CLOTHE ME ANEW

*Put off, concerning your former conduct, the old man which
grows corrupt according to the deceitful lusts, and be renewed in
the spirit of your mind, and . . . put on the new man which was
created according to God, in true righteousness and holiness.*

EPHESIANS 4:22–24

Saving and redeeming Lord, I want to be rid of the dirty clothes
of my "former conduct," of my sinful and corrupt past. I want
to wear instead the snow-white robe of Christ's righteousness.
But only You, Lord, can forgive my failings and sins. Only You can renew
my mind and put on me that new robe, "the new man which was created
according to God, in true righteousness and holiness." Please do that
good work in my life. May I cooperate with Your work in my heart, and
may all the glory go to You! Cover me with the power of Your presence,
that my life will reflect Your glory. I thank You for receiving my prayer.

....

....

....

....

....

....

....

SEEK . . . AND FIND

"I say to you, ask, and it will be given to you; seek, and you will find; knock, and it will be opened to you. For everyone who asks receives, and he who seeks finds, and to him who knocks it will be opened."

LUKE 11:9–10

Compassionate and gracious Father, You invite me to go to You in prayer and seek Your will, and You promise that when I knock, the door "will be opened [to me]." So, Lord, enable me to persevere in my praying, to keep knocking when I lay before You requests from my heart. And please give me wisdom and a keen sensitivity to Your guidance so that I am praying Your will, and then provide me the strength I need to carry out Your will. Grow me into a person of prayer who rejoices in Your presence and revels in the privilege of prayer.

INTERCESSION

I ntercession is a special form of supplication: it is prayer on behalf of those people we care about. What a privilege it is to intercede before God on behalf of other people! Throughout the Old Testament, this type of prayer was the special responsibility of the prophets, and it is a responsibility we believers are to take seriously even today.

There are three types of intercessory prayer. The first is when we see someone with a need and we offer to pray for that person. When we say to someone, "I'll pray for you," we must faithfully follow through and intercede for that individual. We must not use the statement "I'll pray for you" as a polite expression of concern. Our brothers and sisters in Christ count on us to pray for them when we say we will.

Then there are times when the Lord will prompt our spirit to pray for someone. We may not know why or the details involved, but the Holy Spirit does. And as we intercede in obedience to Him, He will give us the words necessary for covering that person with His blessings. What an honor to be used by God in such a way!

Finally, the most significant intercessory prayers are those prayed on our behalf by the Holy Spirit and our Lord, Jesus Christ:

> The Spirit also helps in our weaknesses. For we do not know what we should pray for as we ought, but the Spirit Himself makes intercession for us with groanings which cannot be uttered. Now He who searches the hearts knows what the mind of the Spirit is, because He makes intercession for the saints according to the will of God. (Romans 8:26–27)

When we are asked or prompted to pray for someone—whether a friend or loved one or even a stranger—we must make sure we do so as soon and as willingly as possible. May we let nothing interfere with our prayers for others. May we, in response to God's call, be faithful when we commit to pray for someone in need.

LIVING TO INTERCEDE

[Jesus], because He continues forever, has an unchangeable priesthood. Therefore He is also able to save to the uttermost those who come to God through Him, since He always lives to make intercession for them.

HEBREWS 7:24–25

Lord Jesus, I praise You who live forever, You whose priesthood is unchangeable, You who are able to save anyone who goes to the Father and accepts You as their Savior. And I praise You that Your Spirit is continually available to intercede to my heavenly Father on my behalf. Help me to follow Your example and to intercede in prayer for those who are weak and weary and need Your healing comfort, Your redeeming love, and Your powerful guidance through difficult times. Grow within my heart a sensitive spirit that will not miss any opportunity to openly bring before You the prayer requests of those in need.

JESUS, OUR INTERCESSOR

Who shall bring a charge against God's elect? It is God who justifies. Who is he who condemns? It is Christ who died, and furthermore is also risen, who is even at the right hand of God, who also makes intercession for us.

ROMANS 8:33–34

L ord Jesus, what an encouragement to know that You sit at the right hand of God "[making] intercession for us." Because of Your sacrificial death on the cross and Your resurrection from the grave, I am fully forgiven and fully justified. Grateful for my own salvation, God, I ask You to give me a passion for the lost, for those people who don't yet know You or Your powerful love and forgiveness of their sins. Also grant me compassion for those less fortunate around the world who are suffering in so many ways. And help me to reach out with an unselfish heart—a heart that reflects Your unconditional love.

THE LORD'S INTERCESSION

He shall see the labor of His soul, and be satisfied.
By His knowledge My righteous Servant shall justify many,
For He shall bear their iniquities.
Therefore I will divide Him a portion with the great,
And He shall divide the spoil with the strong,
Because He poured out His soul unto death,
And He was numbered with the transgressors,
And He bore the sin of many,
And made intercession for the transgressors.

ISAIAH 53:11–12

I praise You, Lord Jesus, for bearing my iniquities, for pouring out Your soul unto death as payment for my sins. Lord, from the cross, You "made intercession for the transgressors." Thank You, Jesus, for Your ongoing intercession for me every day. May I be ever mindful of the gift of Your forgiveness, and may my heart of gratitude be one that glorifies You.

THE SPIRIT'S INTERCESSION

*The Spirit also helps in our weaknesses. For we do not know what
we should pray for as we ought, but the Spirit Himself makes
intercession for us with groanings which cannot be uttered. Now He
who searches the hearts knows what the mind of the Spirit is, because
He makes intercession for the saints according to the will of God.*

ROMANS 8:26–27

Attentive and all-wise God, Your Word teaches that Your
"Spirit Himself makes intercession" for me before Your
throne of grace. What comfort and reassurance that truth
gives me, especially during those times when I don't know how or what
to pray. Thank You, Lord God, for providing Your people with an ever-
faithful Intercessor, and for prayers that are "according to the will of
God." And I praise You for the comfort in knowing that, not only do You
intercede on my behalf, but You also walk before me and beside me each
day as I walk in Your presence.

OPENING OUR HEARTS *to* GOD

*"Call to Me, and I will answer you, and show you great and
mighty things, which you do not know."*

JEREMIAH 33:3

God calls each of us to go to Him with all our needs—our
needs for His grace, salvation, love, comfort, hope, and
guidance. Our communication of such needs to the God
of the universe through Scripture and prayer leads to a deeper, richer
relationship with Him, our heavenly Father.

Specifically, through prayer we submit everything to the Lord. In
prayer, we invite God to come into our lives as we ask for His help. When
we obey His commands and place our cares before Him, we relinquish
our control and ask Him to take over any and all areas of concern. This
prayer of submission, this heartfelt step of humbling ourselves before
God and "casting all [our] care upon Him" (1 Peter 5:6–7), pleases God.
Such a prayer is an acknowledgment that God is fully able to take care of
all that concerns us, and that He can do so more thoroughly and more
wisely than we ever could. And this humble approach, this acknowledgment of our finite, sinful human condition, is appropriate whenever we
approach the throne of our holy God.

Now hope does not disappoint, because the love of God has been poured out in our hearts by the Holy Spirit who was given to us.

ROMANS 5:5

SPECIFIC PRAYERS

LOVE

A Father's Love

Behold what manner of love the Father has bestowed on us, that we should be called children of God! Therefore the world does not know us, because it did not know Him. Beloved, now we are children of God; and it has not yet been revealed what we shall be, but we know that when He is revealed, we shall be like Him, for we shall see Him as He is. And everyone who has this hope in Him purifies himself, just as He is pure.

1 JOHN 3:1–3

Father!" What an unbelievable privilege to call You—the eternal I AM, the Creator of all, the Author of history, the Friend and Redeemer of sinners—"Abba, Father." To know that I am Your child—a child of the King of kings—is more wonderful than words can say! As I "behold what manner of love" You have bestowed on me, please teach Me to live in that love, be guided by it, and reflect Your goodness so that others may come to know Your amazing love.

IMMEASURABLE LOVE

God so loved the world that He gave His only begotten Son, that
whoever believes in Him should not perish but have everlasting life.

JOHN 3:16

lmighty and holy God, You "so loved the world" that You gave us the gift of Your "only begotten Son," a gift beyond imagining. I am speechless at the realization that You allowed Jesus to die so that I would have life everlasting. Mindful of Your great sacrifice, Lord God, I long to live each day to bring joy to Your heart and to share the news of Your love with others. I am humbled to be in Your presence, and my heart overflows with gratitude for Your mercy and grace. "Let the words of my mouth and the meditation of my heart be acceptable in Your sight, O LORD, my strength and my Redeemer" (Psalm 19:14).

Unshakeable Love

I am persuaded that neither death nor life, nor angels nor
principalities nor powers, nor things present nor things to come,
nor height nor depth, nor any other created thing, shall be able to
separate us from the love of God which is in Christ Jesus our Lord.

ROMANS 8:38–39

What a ringing pronouncement of a glorious truth, Lord God! Here Your Word proclaims that "neither death nor life . . . nor things present nor things to come, nor height nor depth . . . shall be able to separate us from the love of God, which is in Christ Jesus"! Since You, God, the uncreated One, are *for* me, then it makes sense that no created thing could come between me and Your great love for me. That means I can rest and risk, I can live and dream, I can wake and sleep absolutely secure in You. May I therefore live each day for Your glory. Use me as salt and light in this world that so needs Your love—a love that will never let Your beloved children go.

....

....

....

....

....

....

LOVE'S PROMISES

"A little while longer and the world will see Me no more, but you will see Me. Because I live, you will live also. At that day you will know that I am in My Father, and you in Me, and I in you. He who has My commandments and keeps them, it is he who loves Me. And he who loves Me will be loved by My Father, and I will love him and manifest Myself to him."

JOHN 14:19–21

Lord Jesus, these few verses of Scripture boldly point to Your ascension, celebrate the mysterious blessing of Your Spirit indwelling Your people, and reaffirm the future resurrection of those of us who name You our Savior and Lord. What peace and joy come with these words of promise and this proclamation of Your love for me! Enable me to show my love for You by keeping Your commandments and living each day for Your glory.

Therefore my heart is glad, and my glory rejoices;
    My flesh also will rest in hope. . . .
You will show me the path of life;
    In Your presence is fullness of joy;
    At Your right hand are pleasures
      forevermore.

PSALM 16:9, 11

SPECIFIC PRAYERS

JOY

JOY COMES IN THE MORNING

His anger is but for a moment,
His favor is for life;
Weeping may endure for a night,
But joy comes in the morning.

PSALM 30:5

God of comfort, Giver of joy, I thank You for the favor You bestow on me, "favor [that] is for life." Trouble in my life may prompt weeping, but I know that You are always there to comfort me and that with Your comfort comes the promised joy. So I ask You to keep me ever mindful that the difficulties I encounter on this earth will not last forever. Help me also to share with other children of Yours that the disappointments they face are "but for a moment," for You have promised Your people that "joy comes in the morning."

Rejoicing in Trials

Count it all joy when you fall into various trials, knowing that the testing of your faith produces patience. But let patience have its perfect work, that you may be perfect and complete, lacking nothing.

JAMES 1:2–4

Compassionate and wise Father, no one I know welcomes trials and troubles, and I am certainly no different. When trials come, I can struggle to find joy. So I ask You to allow these trials—this "testing of [my] faith"—to produce patience in me. Grow my trust in You so that I truly can "count it all joy" when hard times come. Purify my heart so that I might have the endurance and patience to live each day for You. My desire is to allow nothing in my life to separate me from Your loving presence.

....

....

....

....

....

....

....

....

Running the Race with Joy

Since we are surrounded by so great a cloud of witnesses, let us lay aside every weight, and the sin which so easily ensnares us, and let us run with endurance the race that is set before us, looking unto Jesus, the author and finisher of our faith, who for the joy that was set before Him endured the cross, despising the shame, and has sat down at the right hand of the throne of God.

HEBREWS 12:1–2

Wise and faithful God, I thank You for enabling those of us who name Jesus as our Savior to endure in our faith. Thank You for the example I find in Jesus: He was able to endure the physical pain, emotional agony, and spiritual darkness of the cross "for the joy that was set before Him." Teach me, Lord Jesus, to keep my eyes on the joy of eternity so I can endure whatever challenges come my way. That great reward of eternal life with You—a reward made possible by Your ultimate sacrifice—is waiting for each of Your children. And as I await that reward, Father, may Your Spirit live within me so that I might become everything You would have me be.

The Joy of Salvation

I have trusted in Your mercy;
My heart shall rejoice in Your salvation.
I will sing to the LORD,
Because He has dealt bountifully with me.

PSALM 13:5–6

Gracious Lord, my heart is indeed filled with joy when I think of my salvation, a gift You paid for with the sacrificial gift of Your Son. I am grateful for other forms of Your love and for the hope of my eternal future with You. When I look back, I clearly see Your mercy and forgiveness shining brightly over every day of my life—You have "dealt bountifully with me"—and I look forward with great anticipation to the future You have planned for me. In the meantime I will—by Your grace—continue to "[trust] in Your mercy" and sing to You, Lord.

....

....

....

....

....

....

....

....

"These things I have spoken to you, that in Me you may have peace. In the world you will have tribulation; but be of good cheer, I have overcome the world."

John 16:33

SPECIFIC
PRAYERS

—⁓⁂⁓—

PEACE

Be Anxious for Nothing

Be anxious for nothing, but in everything by prayer and
supplication, with thanksgiving, let your requests be made known
to God; and the peace of God, which surpasses all understanding,
will guard your hearts and minds through Christ Jesus.

PHILIPPIANS 4:6–7

God of peace, You command me to "be anxious for nothing," and—as You already know—that is not easy for me to do. Many times I worry about things I cannot control. I know Your Word tells me to pray about everything "with thanksgiving" and to "let [my] requests be made known to [You]." So please take away from me the prideful desire I have to solve my problems on my own. Instead, help me to look to You in all my circumstances. Even today, right at this moment, I open my heart to You to receive the promise of Your peace "which surpasses all understanding," peace You will use to guard my heart and mind as I learn to trust more fully in the love of Christ Jesus.

A GIFT FROM JESUS

"Peace I leave with you, My peace I give to you; not as the world gives do I give to you. Let not your heart be troubled, neither let it be afraid."

JOHN 14:27

L ord Jesus my Good Shepherd, You know what Your followers need, and You meet those needs. You also know the human yearning for peace. Not peace "as the world gives," but Your peace. I can't know Your peace, though, when I try to solve every problem on my own, when I neglect to go to You for the solutions and the guidance that only You can give. Yet any peace "the world gives" cannot compare to the perfect peace I find in You. In You alone, Jesus, will my heart not be troubled or afraid. After all, the peace You give can overcome any fear I may have, and I thank You for revealing that truth to me.

....

....

....

....

....

....

....

....

CHRIST, OUR PEACE

[Jesus] Himself is our peace, who has made both [Gentiles and Jews] one, and has broken down the middle wall of separation, having abolished in His flesh the enmity, that is, the law of commandments contained in ordinances, so as to create in Himself one new man from the two, thus making peace.

EPHESIANS 2:14–15

Lord Jesus, You are my peace. The forgiveness of my sin that You secured on the cross made possible the peace that now exists between You, my holy Creator God, and me. Because Your sacrifice satisfied the law's requirement that blood cover my sin, I know peace with God. I give thanks that this peace allows me to have a close and intimate relationship with You each and every day. Draw me even closer to You that I might live in Your presence, reflecting Your glory, and prompting people to pursue You.

....

....

....

....

....

....

....

THE PEACE OF GOD

Let the peace of God rule in your hearts, to which also you were called in one body; and be thankful. Let the word of Christ dwell in you richly in all wisdom, teaching and admonishing one another in psalms and hymns and spiritual songs, singing with grace in your hearts to the Lord.

COLOSSIANS 3:15–16

Almighty God, You long to have Your peace "rule in [the] hearts" of Your people, yet I am well aware that I don't always cooperate. I choose to worry rather than focus on You. I fill my time and my mind with sounds of this world rather than with "psalms and hymns and spiritual songs." No wonder I feel unsettled, uneasy, unrooted. I neglect to "let the word of Christ dwell in [me] richly." No wonder I'm low on wisdom. With my focus on the activities and noise of this world, no wonder I don't find myself "singing with grace . . . to the Lord." Please change my focus, change my song, that my life may be characterized by my gratitude for You and Your many blessings.

UNITY AND PEACE

Walk worthy of the calling with which you were called . . .
endeavoring to keep the unity of the Spirit in the bond of peace.
There is one body and one Spirit, just as you were called in one
hope of your calling; one Lord, one faith, one baptism; one God
and Father of all, who is above all, and through all, and in you all.

EPHESIANS 4:1, 3–6

L ord of love, it's been said that the world will know we are Your people by the love we have for one another. No wonder You call us—You command us—to "keep the unity of the Spirit in the bond of peace." I ask You to help me make every effort toward that end. For "there is one body and one Spirit . . . one Lord, one faith," and I thank You for opening my eyes to that truth. So, as I walk with You through each day, please enable me, moment by moment, to choose to depend on Your Spirit so You can use me to be a peacemaker and a bridge builder.

....

....

....

....

....

....

THE POWERFUL GOD OF PEACE

May the God of peace who brought up our Lord Jesus from the dead, that great Shepherd of the sheep, through the blood of the everlasting covenant, make you complete in every good work to do His will, working in you what is well pleasing in His sight, through Jesus Christ, to whom be glory forever and ever. Amen.

HEBREWS 13:20–21

Sovereign and all-powerful Lord, Your Word describes You as "the God of peace." You enable sinners to be at peace with You who are holy. And, by the power of Your Spirit, You enable sinners to be at peace with one another. So, in response to Jesus' death for my sin—in response to "the blood of the everlasting covenant" that spilled from His body as He hung on the cross—I want to do good works according to Your will. I want to live in a way that is "well pleasing in [Your] sight." I ask You to use me, Almighty God, to honor and glorify Your Son, the One "to whom be glory forever and ever." For You, O Lord, are greatly to be praised.

Give us this day our daily bread.
  And forgive us our debts,
  As we forgive our debtors.
  And do not lead us into temptation,
  But deliver us from the evil one.
  For Yours is the kingdom and the power and
    the glory forever. Amen.

Matthew 6:11–13

SPECIFIC PRAYERS

—⁓⁂⁓—

TEMPTATION

Victory over Temptation

No temptation has overtaken you except such as is common to man; but God is faithful, who will not allow you to be tempted beyond what you are able, but with the temptation will also make the way of escape, that you may be able to bear it.

1 Corinthians 10:13

ood and powerful Lord, in Your Word, the apostle Paul boldly declared that "no temptation has overtaken [him] except [those that are] common" to everyone. I thank You for the promise that follows that statement: You are faithful to always provide a way of escape. O Lord, if only I would consistently choose to resist temptation. Prompt in me, Lord, not only an instant recognition of temptations as they arise but also the immediate godly response of seeking Your protection, Your guidance to the "way of escape," and Your Spirit's power to choose that way.

A WILLING SPIRIT

"Watch and pray, lest you enter into temptation. The spirit indeed is willing, but the flesh is weak."

MATTHEW 26:41

O Lord Jesus, human nature hasn't changed. My spirit is indeed willing to spend more time with You—to fast and pray, to memorize Scripture, to serve in a way that is out of my comfort zone. Yes, my spirit "is willing, but the flesh is weak," very weak. I need Your strength so that I can live each day for You, in obedience to Your Spirit, standing strong against temptation, clinging to Your power over the enemy.

STRENGTH TO ENDURE

Blessed is the man who endures temptation; for when he has been approved, he will receive the crown of life which the Lord has promised to those who love Him. Let no one say when he is tempted, "I am tempted by God"; for God cannot be tempted by evil, nor does He Himself tempt anyone.

JAMES 1:12–13

James is right: "Blessed is the man who endures temptation." And, O Lord, how I need You to help me do exactly that! The enemy knows my weaknesses; he knows the places where I am vulnerable. But I know You, and I know that Your Spirit will give me the strength to overcome whatever temptation comes my way.

....

....

....

....

....

....

....

....

THE LORD IS FAITHFUL

The Lord is faithful, who will establish you and guard you from the evil one.

2 THESSALONIANS 3:3

J esus was clear: in this world we will face trials and temptations (John 16:33). Life in this fallen world, the life of this child of God living among sinners, is fraught with pain, challenges, disappointment, loss, and temptation. Since the journey of life is anything but easy and pain-free, I am thankful that You are "faithful [to] establish [me] and guard [me] from the evil one." In the name of Jesus, I therefore rebuke Satan and declare that he has no power over me because I am Yours. With heartfelt gratitude, I praise You, Lord!

Your righteousness, O God, is very high,
  You who have done great things;
  O God, who is like You? . . .

You shall increase my greatness,
  And comfort me on every side.

PSALM 71:19, 21

SPECIFIC PRAYERS

COMFORT

My Refuge, My Fortress

He who dwells in the secret place of the Most High
Shall abide under the shadow of the Almighty.
I will say of the Lord, "He is my refuge and my fortress;
My God, in Him I will trust."

Psalm 91:1–2

What a privileged dwelling place—"in the secret place of the Most High . . . under the shadow of the Almighty"! Thank You that, when the winds of life are gale force, when the shaky ground of the world's ways trembles, when other people's free will causes complications or pain, I can run to You! I praise You for the times You have indeed been my refuge and my fortress. I praise You for Your faithfulness and for the countless ways You have grown my trust in You. May I proclaim with my decisions, with my very life, the truth that You are faithful and good, that You are "my refuge and my fortress." Help me to trust You even in my weakest moments, for You are the God of my salvation and nothing is too hard for You.

....

....

....

....

....

....

THE GOD OF ALL COMFORT

Blessed be the God and Father of our Lord Jesus Christ, the Father of mercies and God of all comfort, who comforts us in all our tribulation, that we may be able to comfort those who are in any trouble, with the comfort with which we ourselves are comforted by God.

2 CORINTHIANS 1:3–4

Compassionate and loving Father, You have indeed been and continue to be the "God of all comfort." You have always comforted me in my tribulation and heartbreak. And I thank You, Lord, that one way You redeem that pain is by enabling me to come alongside others who are hurting, to share "the comfort with which [I am] comforted by God," and to point them to You. Help me be sensitive to people around me who need strength. Give me Your eyes so that I will see people who need comfort. Then use me as a vessel of Your compassion to be a blessing—to them. My greatest desire is to serve You faithfully.

HIS ETERNAL PERSPECTIVE

"Let not your heart be troubled; you believe in God, believe also in Me. In My Father's house are many mansions; if it were not so, I would have told you. I go to prepare a place for you. And if I go and prepare a place for you, I will come again and receive you to Myself; that where I am, there you may be also."

JOHN 14:1–3

Lord Jesus, You walked this earth. You know the troubles that abound here. So You undoubtedly know as well the joy Your promise brings. "I go to prepare a place for you" lifts my eyes beyond the world I see to the very real eternity with You that awaits. What a source of comfort that perspective is! And what a comfort to know that You have prepared a place for me in Your heavenly kingdom!

....

....

....

....

....

....

....

He Cares for You

Humble yourselves under the mighty hand of God, that He may exalt you in due time, casting all your care upon Him, for He cares for you.

1 PETER 5:6–7

You are indeed the Almighty God, the Creator of the universe, and the Sustainer of life. Nothing is impossible for You! And how helpful it is for me to step back from my concerns, and to remind myself of who my infinite God is. In awe and gratitude, I humbly come before You and lay at Your feet all my worries and anxieties, all my problems and concerns. We who are Your people know that You are the God of all comfort, and I know that what Peter wrote is true: You care for me. Thank You, my good and gracious God.

....

....

....

....

....

....

....

....

....

"But to you who fear My name
    The Sun of Righteousness shall arise
    With healing in His wings;
    And you shall go out
    And grow fat like stall-fed calves.
You shall trample the wicked,
    For they shall be ashes under the soles of
        your feet
    On the day that I do this,"
    Says the LORD of hosts.

MALACHI 4:2–3

SPECIFIC PRAYERS

—⁂—

HEALING

Lord, Heal Me

The Lord will strengthen him on his bed of illness;
You will sustain him on his sickbed.
I said, "Lord, be merciful to me;
Heal my soul, for I have sinned against You."

Psalm 41:3–4

Most gracious Lord, come to me in my time of illness. You are Jehovah Rapha, the great and mighty Healer, and I ask that You heal me so that I might rise up and serve You. Be merciful to me, O Lord, and bless me with health so that I am able to bless others with acts of service and care. If it is Your will, take this sickness from me and strengthen my spirit as well as my body for Your glory.

EFFECTIVE, FERVENT PRAYER

The prayer of faith will save the sick, and the Lord will raise him up. And if he has committed sins, he will be forgiven. Confess your trespasses to one another, and pray for one another, that you may be healed. The effective, fervent prayer of a righteous man avails much.

JAMES 5:15–16

F ather, You promise that "the prayer of faith will save the sick." I know that my sins can block my prayers, so please open my heart and mind so that I am able to acknowledge and confess my wrongdoings, experience Your forgiveness and mercy, and be empowered to pray effectively for others. Only in Your strength can I remain fervent in prayer and anticipate Your promise of healing. I trust that Your will and the timing of Your healing touch will be perfect.

....

....

....

....

....

....

....

A Cry for Healing

Have mercy on me, O LORD, for I am weak;
O LORD, heal me, for my bones are troubled.
My soul also is greatly troubled;
But You, O LORD—how long?

PSALM 6:2–3

Merciful and powerful God, I need Your healing. My body is weak, I have little energy, and my spirits are low. I long to regain my health. So I cry out to You for mercy—for Your healing touch and for strength to endure. Please take this illness from me. I long to continue to serve You and tell others of Your marvelous mercy and grace. I thank You for Your faithfulness and for listening to my plea.

Jesus' Ultimate Sacrifice

He was wounded for our transgressions,
He was bruised for our iniquities;
The chastisement for our peace was upon Him,
And by His stripes we are healed.

ISAIAH 53:5

L ord Jesus, even when I find myself longing for physical healing for others or for myself, I rejoice that You provided the
ultimate spiritual healing for all of mankind. You received
no political justice, Your friends deserted and betrayed You, You were
flogged and mocked, and You were nailed to a cross. You shed Your
blood, You experienced utter separation from Your heavenly Father, and
You died—all so that sinners like me can be saved from the consequences
of our sin, forgiven for those sins, and welcomed into a relationship with
our heavenly Father. As the prophet said, You were "wounded for our
transgressions . . . bruised for our iniquities . . . and by [Your] stripes we
are healed." Jesus, may my mindfulness of Your indescribable sacrifice
keep me humble in Your presence and a humble servant in this world.

Praise the Lord!

> *Blessed is the man who fears the Lord,*
> *Who delights greatly in His commandments.*

His descendants will be mighty on earth;
> *The generation of the upright will be blessed.*
Wealth and riches will be in his house,
> *And his righteousness endures forever.*

Psalm 112:1–3

SPECIFIC PRAYERS

FINANCIAL NEEDS

I WILL CARRY YOU

"Listen to Me, O house of Jacob,
And all the remnant of the house of Israel,
Who have been upheld by Me from birth,
Who have been carried from the womb:
Even to your old age, I am He,
And even to gray hairs I will carry you!
I have made, and I will bear;
Even I will carry, and will deliver you."

ISAIAH 46:3–4

Gracious and generous God, You are the Giver of all good gifts. You know my needs before I bring them to You. And You who have faithfully "carried [me] from the womb" promise to continue to carry me and deliver me through any problems I may encounter. Right now, Lord, I ask for deliverance from difficult financial issues that You are well aware of. Lord, I know that this apparently impossible situation is not impossible for You, that You are sovereign and wise and good, so I ask You for wisdom and to deliver me—and to You be all the glory! Deliver me, I pray, that I may faithfully serve You in all things.

LORD, I NEED YOU

Save now, I pray, O LORD;
O LORD, I pray, send now prosperity.
Blessed is he who comes in the name of the LORD!
We have blessed you from the house of the LORD.

PSALM 118:25–26

Dear Father, You who are gracious and kind, hear my prayer! I face more financial pressure than I can bear. "Save [me] now, I pray." Show me, Lord, what I must do to get out from under this heavy burden. Give me Your wisdom and discipline, I pray, that I may move toward resolution of this situation. Guard my heart, Lord, and my steps; protect me from bad advice and foolish actions. Draw me close to You, for I need Your comfort and guidance.

WALKING IN TRUTH

Beloved, I pray that you may prosper in all things and be in health,
just as your soul prospers. For I rejoiced greatly when brethren came
and testified of the truth that is in you, just as you walk in the truth.
I have no greater joy than to hear that my children walk in truth.

3 JOHN 2–4

Thank You for Your Word, Lord God. Thank You for its message of truth and encouragement. I am especially encouraged today by the apostle John's words that reflect Your fatherly love: "I pray that you may prosper in all things." Give me the courage, Lord, to be a faithful steward of all that You have entrusted to me. Enable me to wisely untangle current financial knots. Most of all, even as I address today's financial needs, help me to look beyond them, to walk in Your truth, and to rejoice in the hope of eternity with You.

FASTING AND PRAYING

I set my face toward the Lord God to make request by prayer and supplications, with fasting, sackcloth, and ashes. And I prayed to the LORD my God, and made confession, and said, "O Lord, great and awesome God, who keeps His covenant and mercy with those who love Him, and with those who keep His commandments."

DANIEL 9:3–4

Sometimes we become sharply aware of our sin. Sometimes danger looms or an important decision must be made. Sometimes we are burdened by a weary heart. Various circumstances like these can compel us to set our face toward God with a renewed focus. And fasting is a long-standing discipline by which we can do exactly that. Simply put, fasting is abstaining from something—usually food—for spiritual reasons. Fasting is a means of intentionally pursuing the God of heaven, of focusing on Him instead of our material or physical needs, of listening for His direction, and of petitioning Him for something near and dear to our hearts.

Daniel knew the value of fasting, and we can learn from his example. He recognized that God's people had strayed far from His ways, and he was desperate for God to move among them, to prompt the children of Israel to repent of their sins and reestablish a life that reflected their commitment to God. So Daniel humbled himself before the Lord in prayer and fasting.

And this is not just an Old Testament practice. Jesus Himself spoke to His followers about "when you fast," not *if* (Matthew 6:17).

When we seek God through fasting, we can see Him work in wonderful ways. Prayer joined by fasting creates an incomparable intimacy with our Lord. As we experience our relationship with God at this deeper, richer level, our prayers can become more effective than ever.

SPECIFIC PRAYERS

OBEDIENCE
AND
BLESSING

Desiring to Please God

Be strong and very courageous, that you may observe to do according to all the law which Moses My servant commanded you; do not turn from it to the right hand or to the left, that you may prosper wherever you go. This Book of the Law shall not depart from your mouth, but you shall meditate in it day and night, that you may observe to do according to all that is written in it. For then you will make your way prosperous, and then you will have good success.

JOSHUA 1:7–8

Wise Father and reigning Lord, all of Your commands are for my good and Your glory, yet too often I want to do life my way. Please work in my heart so that I desire to please You more than I desire to please myself. Put simply, place in me a desire to obey You. Keep me meditating on Your Word and relying on the power of the Holy Spirit "that [I] may observe to do according to all that is written in it." My deepest desire is to glorify You, Lord, and may any blessings of prosperity and success You grant me bring You great glory.

LIVING AS CHRIST'S SLAVE

He who is called in the Lord while a slave is the Lord's freedman. Likewise he who is called while free is Christ's slave. You were bought at a price; do not become slaves of men. Brethren, let each one remain with God in that state in which he was called.

1 CORINTHIANS 7:22–24

Almighty God, I was "bought at a price," at the indescribable price of Your only Son's death on a cross. Mindful of that, may I—with Your help—be faithful to Your calling on my life. May I be Your faithful servant, "Christ's slave," in the very place where You have me today. Please give me eyes to see opportunities to serve at home and in the workplace, in my neighborhood and in my church. Remove my selfish desires and any longing for man's approval and praise. I want, Lord God, to live in the center of Your will so that You will be glorified in my life.

TEACH ME YOUR STATUTES

Blessed are You, O Lord!
Teach me Your statutes.
With my lips I have declared
All the judgments of Your mouth.
I have rejoiced in the way of Your testimonies,
As much as in all riches.
I will meditate on Your precepts,
And contemplate Your ways.
I will delight myself in Your statutes;
I will not forget Your word.

PSALM 119:12–16

Father God and King of kings, I long to live in obedience to Your statutes and commands. In order to do so, enable me to "meditate on Your precepts" that they will direct my steps. As I "contemplate Your ways," give me a keen awareness of the guidance I can find there. Teach me, I pray, to live in a way that pleases You and gives You glory.

GIVE ME UNDERSTANDING

Deal with Your servant according to Your mercy,
And teach me Your statutes.
I am Your servant;
Give me understanding,
That I may know Your testimonies.

PSALM 119:124–125

L ord of lords, "I am Your servant," and I am a stumbling servant. Too often I fall short of Your standards. Too often I choose not to seek Your will; too often I choose not to love with Your love. So, yes, please deal with me "according to Your mercy," but don't stop there! Lord, please "teach me Your statutes . . . [and] give me understanding" so that the guidelines and truths found in Your Word may lodge in my heart and direct my steps. Continue, I pray, to fuel my desire to obey You and continue to increase my understanding of both Your Word and what obedience looks like. I look forward each day to living in Your presence and having a loving relationship with You. Your Word is a priceless treasure that gives me a beacon of light to be obedient to my calling.

For the Son of Man has come to save that which was lost.

MATTHEW 18:11

SPECIFIC PRAYERS

THE LOST

AND

UNSAVED

GRACE AND GRATITUDE

By grace you have been saved through faith, and that not of yourselves; it is the gift of God, not of works, lest anyone should boast. For we are His workmanship, created in Christ Jesus for good works, which God prepared beforehand that we should walk in them.

EPHESIANS 2:8–10

God of truth and light, I thank You for the priceless gift of salvation. Because of the sacrifice of Your Son, because of His death on the cross, my sins are forgiven, I am no longer separated from you—I am blessed to be in relationship with You now and for eternity. Create in me the desire to serve You faithfully, that I may do the "good works . . . [that You] prepared beforehand" for me. And may I also share with others the reason for my hope, the reason that I serve—the gift of faith in Jesus Christ, my Savior. Help me Lord to walk in step with You each and every day, that I might reflect the love You have promised.

GOD'S CHOSEN PEOPLE

You are a chosen generation, a royal priesthood, a holy nation, His own special people, that you may proclaim the praises of Him who called you out of darkness into His marvelous light; who once were not a people but are now the people of God, who had not obtained mercy but now have obtained mercy.

1 PETER 2:9–10

When I think, holy and sovereign Lord, that You chose me to be a member of "a royal priesthood, a holy nation," I am humbled and grateful. May I therefore "proclaim [Your] praises" with my words and deeds, especially when I have the opportunity to introduce You to someone who is not yet walking in Your mercy and grace. I thank You for calling me "out of darkness into [Your] marvelous light." Please use me to do the same for people still in darkness.

GOD'S PROMISE FOR ALL

God so loved the world that He gave His only begotten Son, that whoever believes in Him should not perish but have everlasting life. For God did not send His Son into the world to condemn the world, but that the world through Him might be saved.

JOHN 3:16–17

God of love and God of all, You make it no secret. You so love the world that You were willing to give Your "only begotten Son, that whoever believes in Him should not perish but have everlasting life." How can I thank You for helping me recognize Jesus as Your Son, my Savior! And this great love of Yours is not restricted to any single nation or any spiritually elite group. You sent Jesus "that the world through Him might be saved"! Here I am, Lord, willing to be used for that divine purpose. Help me each day to share Your mercy and grace that others might be blessed to come to know You and Your saving grace.

Heirs in God's Family

You are all sons of God through faith in Christ Jesus. For as many of you as were baptized into Christ have put on Christ. There is neither Jew nor Greek, there is neither slave nor free, there is neither male nor female; for you are all one in Christ Jesus. And if you are Christ's, then you are Abraham's seed, and heirs according to the promise.

GALATIANS 3:26–29

Thank You, kind and gracious Father, for adopting me into Your family. As a child "of God through faith in Christ Jesus," I am blessed and privileged to be able to say that I belong to You. But, I ask, please teach me more and more what it means to "put on Christ," that I may honor You in all I do. Lord, one way I do want to honor You is by reaching out to, figuratively speaking, both Jew and Greek, both slave and free, both male and female, so that they, too, can place their faith in Jesus and know You as their heavenly Father.

THE MINISTRY OF RECONCILIATION

If anyone is in Christ, he is a new creation; old things have passed away; behold, all things have become new. Now all things are of God, who has reconciled us to Himself through Jesus Christ, and has given us the ministry of reconciliation, that is, that God was in Christ reconciling the world to Himself, not imputing their trespasses to them, and has committed to us the word of reconciliation.

2 CORINTHIANS 5:17–19

All-powerful, all-good God, what an amazing blesssing to have become "a new creation" when I named Jesus as my Savior and Lord! And the news of this transformation and fresh start is too good to keep to myself. As I live in Your presence and walk closely with You, show me with whom and how to share this news of salvation. I want You to use me in "the ministry of reconciliation," that people I encounter according to Your divine appointments may come to know the joy and hope of being a new creation in Christ Jesus.

ALL HAVE SINNED

All have sinned and fall short of the glory of God, being justified
freely by His grace through the redemption that is in Christ Jesus,
whom God set forth as a propitiation by His blood, through faith,
to demonstrate His righteousness, because in His forbearance
God had passed over the sins that were previously committed, to
demonstrate at the present time His righteousness, that He might
be just and the justifier of the one who has faith in Jesus.

ROMANS 3:23–26

Holy God, Your Word clearly teaches that "all have sinned and fall short of the glory of God." I know too well my own sin nature—the appeal of sin, the ease with which I fall into sinful ways, the difficulty I have controlling my tongue, and the list goes on. By Your grace, however, I have experienced "the redemption that is in Christ Jesus," Your only Son, whom You sent as a blood sacrifice to cover my sins. I praise You for Your forgiveness, yet may I never forget the sin from which You have delivered me. May that awareness of my sin keep me humble when I share with people what it is to know Jesus as Savior and Lord.

Give to the Lord the glory due His name;
Bring an offering, and come before Him.
Oh, worship the Lord in the beauty of
holiness!

1 Chronicles 16:29

SPECIFIC PRAYERS

—◦❧◦•◦—

WORSHIP

A Call to Worship

*Oh come, let us sing to the L*ORD*!*
Let us shout joyfully to the Rock of our salvation.
Let us come before His presence with thanksgiving;
Let us shout joyfully to Him with psalms.
*For the L*ORD *is the great God,*
And the great King above all gods. . . .
Oh come, let us worship and bow down;
*Let us kneel before the L*ORD *our Maker.*
For He is our God,
And we are the people of His pasture,
And the sheep of His hand.

PSALM 95:1–3, 6–7

What an amazing invitation! You, my holy God, invite me, a sinner, to enter into Your presence, to humbly "bow down," to "shout joyfully," to worship You. All glory to You, my Maker, my God, my great and mighty King. I am blessed to be one of Your people, a sheep in Your flock. And You, my faithful Shepherd, grant me grace, mercy, and forgiveness when I fail You. May that reality fuel in me a lifetime of heartfelt worship!

Exalt the Lord

Exalt the LORD our God,
And worship at His footstool—
He is holy. . . .
Exalt the LORD our God,
And worship at His holy hill;
For the LORD our God is holy.

PSALM 99:5, 9

Risen Jesus, according to an early hymn, one day every knee will bow and every tongue confess that You are Lord (Philippians 2:10–11). I am blessed to already have the joy of recognizing that truth and worshipping You! Entering Your presence to exalt and worship You is a privilege! And when I do come before You, to "worship at [Your] footstool," You make it a blessing and a source of comfort to my soul. So I lift my hands high and praise Your holy name! I worship You, my glorious God, for such blessings as Your forgiveness, Your unconditional love, Your faithfulness, and Your guidance. I ask You, the One who gives my life purpose, to teach me how to worship You wherever I am, and whatever I'm doing.

A Song of Praise

Make a joyful shout to God, all the earth!
Sing out the honor of His name;
Make His praise glorious.
Say to God,
"How awesome are Your works!
Through the greatness of Your power
Your enemies shall submit themselves to You.
All the earth shall worship You
And sing praises to You;
They shall sing praises to Your name."

PSALM 66:1–4

What a privilege, Almighty God, to join with the psalmist and "sing out the honor of [Your] name"! You deserve glorious praise for Your awesome works, for Your great power, for Your grace and mercy and love. You are more wonderful than words can express! Lord, You created me to praise You—and what joy I find in doing exactly that! I kneel before You now and worship You in truth and sincerity. Your name is to be praised!

....

....

....

....

....

GIVING GOD GLORY

Give unto the LORD, O you mighty ones,
Give unto the LORD glory and strength.

PSALM 29:1

Teach me, I pray, to glorify You, my King and my God, in every area of my life. You are gracious and generous, faithful and wise. I worship You in the beauty of Your holiness. Your compassion is everlasting, and Your love never fails. Touch me, I pray, that Your loving Spirit will guide my steps that I might live every moment in Your presence. For You, O Lord, are greatly to be praised for all You do and for all that You are!

....

....

....

....

....

....

....

....

....

God Listens to Your Hearts

You understand my thought afar off.
You comprehend my path and my lying down,
And are acquainted with all my ways.
For there is not a word on my tongue,
But behold, O LORD, You know it altogether.

PSALM 139:2–4

*P*onder the wondrous truth of the psalmist's words, and find comfort in them!

God is your Creator, your *Abba* Father, your Judge, your King. As such, He knows the outward things that people can know—your strengths, abilities, and accomplishments. But He also knows the inward things—your desires, hopes, and dreams. He is aware of how you feel, and He knows your unspoken needs and hidden hurts. He knows what thrills your soul and what breaks your heart. He who knit you together in your mother's womb knows you completely, and He pays attention to every detail of your life. God knows everything about you. He knows your past, your present, and, yes, your future. He hears your spoken words as well as the unspoken words of your heart, and still He loves you!

In response to this incomprehensible, heaven-sent love, may we believers love the Lord with an urgency, a fervor, a zealous desire to both know Him better and glorify Him more fully. May we respond with a life characterized by prayer, by continual communication with our heavenly Father. Truly knowing the Lord comes only by spending time with Him in prayer (that means listening for His voice as well as speaking to Him) and delving deeper into His Word. And it is easier and wiser to entrust your heart to Someone you know well and trust completely.

SPECIFIC PRAYERS

—⁓⁓—

HOPE

FINDING HOPE IN JESUS' LOVE

*Behold what manner of love the Father has bestowed on us, that
we should be called children of God! . . . Beloved, now we are
children of God; . . . we know that when He is revealed, we shall
be like Him, for we shall see Him as He is. And everyone who has
this hope in Him purifies himself, just as He is pure.*

1 JOHN 3:1–3

Father God, I behold with amazement and awe "what manner
of love [You have] bestowed on us"! As if the love revealed
in Your works of forgiveness and salvation and sanctifica-
tion aren't blessing enough, You go a step further: "that we should be
called children of God"! This new status—and this act of pure grace,
this astounding evidence of Your amazing love—fills me with heartfelt
joy and solid hope for the present as well as the future. I want to live in
the power of Your presence. Lord purify my heart just as You are pure.

In Praise of Trust and Hope

You are my hope, O Lord God;
You are my trust from my youth.
By You I have been upheld from birth;
You are He who took me out of my mother's womb.
My praise shall be continually of You. . . .
My mouth shall tell of Your righteousness
And Your salvation all the day,
For I do not know their limits.

PSALM 71:5–6, 15

Almighty God and heavenly Father, You "took me out of my mother's womb." You have "upheld [me] from birth." You have been with me all of my days, guiding me to a saving knowledge of Jesus, forgiving my sins, teaching me to trust You, and blessing me with the promise of spending eternity with You. The joy of knowing You and the joy of seeing Your faithfulness to me through the years fills me with hope day and night. And may that theme of hope be unmistakable whenever I "tell of Your righteousness and Your salvation," whenever I share about Your saving grace with those who don't yet know You. The world is hungry for hope. Enable me to share hope in You effectively and lovingly.

HOPE THAT DOES NOT DISAPPOINT

Having been justified by faith, we have peace with God through our Lord Jesus Christ, through whom also we have access by faith into this grace in which we stand, and rejoice in hope of the glory of God. And not only that, but we also glory in tribulations, knowing that tribulation produces perseverance; and perseverance, character; and character, hope. Now hope does not disappoint, because the love of God has been poured out in our hearts by the Holy Spirit who was given to us.

ROMANS 5:1–5

How grateful I am, eternal God and Father, for the big-picture perspective I find in Your Word. However challenging life is, I "have peace with God through [my] Lord Jesus Christ." And however painful those challenges are, they are worth the pain. I can "glory in [the trials and] tribulations" You allow to come into my life because You use them to teach me perseverance, to build in me the character You wish to see in my life, and to bless me with "hope [that] does not disappoint." Lord, in all circumstances, draw me closer to You so that I may reflect Your glory and share with others the hope available in You.

....

....

....

....

HIS COMPASSION IS NEW EVERY MORNING

Through the LORD's mercies we are not consumed,
Because His compassions fail not.
They are new every morning;
Great is Your faithfulness.
"The LORD is my portion," says my soul,
"Therefore I hope in Him!"

LAMENTATIONS 3:22–24

Compassionate and gracious Lord, life in this broken world is difficult and painful, but because of Your mercies I am "not consumed." Your compassion enables me to get out of bed each day despite the headlines. I praise You for Your mercy and compassion which is "new every morning." Your faithfulness to Your people through time and eternity and Your faithfulness to me through the years of my life give me solid reason to have hope in You and Your sovereign power. This day and every day may I discover anew Your grace and love and find them to be yet another reason to hope in You. Guide me to live in the center of Your will that You might be lifted up. Praise Your holy name.

He heals the brokenhearted
  And binds up their wounds.
He counts the number of the stars;
  He calls them all by name.
Great is our Lord, and mighty in power;
  His understanding is infinite.

PSALM 147:3–5

SPECIFIC
PRAYERS

PRAYERS
FOR THE
BROKENHEARTED

THE LORD IS NEAR

The LORD is near to those who have a broken heart,
And saves such as have a contrite spirit.
Many are the afflictions of the righteous,
But the LORD delivers him out of them all.

PSALM 34:18–19

All-knowing, ever-compassionate Lord, You know without my saying so: my heart is broken. I'm wondering how I got to this point and where to go from here, what I did to contribute to this situation and what I can learn from it. I wrestle with these questions between waves of grief. But when the grief overwhelms and I can't see past the afflictions of the moment, cover me with Your Spirit and deliver me from the anguish that fills my heart. Help me to rest in your loving arms. May Your presence with me—may the nearness of my Deliverer and Redeemer—make answers to my questions unimportant. May Your presence with me be enough. Open my eyes to Your loving comfort and Your blessings so that I may once again find joy in my heart.

....

....

....

....

....

....

HEALING FOR THE BROKENHEARTED

"The Spirit of the LORD is upon Me,
Because He has anointed Me
To preach the gospel to the poor;
He has sent Me to heal the brokenhearted,
To proclaim liberty to the captives
And recovery of sight to the blind,
To set at liberty those who are oppressed;
To proclaim the acceptable year of the LORD."

LUKE 4:18–19

Early in Your ministry, Lord, You boldly proclaimed that God had anointed You to "heal the brokenhearted." I am one of those, Jesus. My heart is broken, and I need Your comforting presence and healing touch. Please take away the pain within me and replace it with Your healing balm. Set me free from the torment of soul and spirit. As You promised, please heal my broken heart.

....

....

....

....

....

....

*But the Lord is faithful, who will establish you
and guard you from the evil one.*

2 THESSALONIANS 3:3

SPECIFIC PRAYERS

PROTECTION

GOD'S RIGHTEOUS RIGHT HAND

"Fear not, for I am with you;
Be not dismayed, for I am your God.
I will strengthen you,
Yes, I will help you,
I will uphold you with My righteous right hand."

ISAIAH 41:10

Lord of heaven and Lord of earth, everywhere I turn I see problems and circumstances beyond my control. I see threats and uncertainties. I am very aware that I need Your protection—and this wonderful truth from Your prophet Isaiah reminds me that You provide exactly that. "Fear not" is a tough command to obey, but the "I am with you" promise makes it easier. So I claim Your promises of strength and help as well as Your promise to "uphold [me] with [Your] righteous right hand." I thank You for being my God, for being with me, and for the strength and help that I find in Your very presence.

WHOM SHALL I FEAR?

The LORD is my light and my salvation;
Whom shall I fear?
The LORD is the strength of my life;
Of whom shall I be afraid?
When the wicked came against me
To eat up my flesh,
My enemies and foes,
They stumbled and fell.
Though an army may encamp against me,
My heart shall not fear;
Though war may rise against me,
In this I will be confident.

PSALM 27:1–3

O f whom shall I be afraid?" May the psalmist's cry of faith be mine as well, Almighty God, You who are "my light and my salvation." Because You are all-powerful and always with me, I need not be afraid of the enemy. Yes, enemies, foes, and wickedness are realities in this world. But the vivid images of this song of praise remind me of Your power and of the truth that I can be confident and unafraid because You are "the strength of my life."

....

....

....

....

Fear Not!

"Fear not, for I have redeemed you;
I have called you by your name;
You are Mine.
When you pass through the waters, I will be with you;
And through the rivers, they shall not overflow you.
When you walk through the fire, you shall not be burned,
Nor shall the flame scorch you.
For I am the LORD your God,
The Holy One of Israel, your Savior."

ISAIAH 43:1–3

What great comfort comes with knowing that You, eternal and omnipotent God of the universe, "have called [me] by . . . name" and that I belong to You. The boldness of Your declaration "You are Mine" gives me a solid sense of security. I know You will be with me no matter what comes along in life. Yes, rising waters and flames of fire are realities, but so is Your ongoing protection. May my remembrances of Your love and care as well as my awareness of Your promise to be with me help me to be strong in my faith and steadfast in living each day.

....

....

....

....

MY GREAT PROTECTOR

Now to Him who is able to keep you from stumbling,
And to present you faultless
Before the presence of His glory with exceeding joy,
To God our Savior,
Who alone is wise,
Be glory and majesty,
Dominion and power,
Both now and forever.
Amen.

JUDE VV. 24–25

You know I am but dust, merciful Lord. So You are not surprised by my human limitations, my failings, or my sins. You are not surprised that I need You "to keep [me] from stumbling" and "to present [me] faultless before the presence of [Your] glory." And just as You protect me from those external forces that distract and trip me up, please protect me from my inner sinful nature and from my own bad choices that would cause me to stumble. Continue to hold me tight and keep me from falling down. And, Lord, I ask You to change me from the inside out that I might reflect Your glory, the glory of my Great Protector.

....

....

....

....

THE GOD WHO HEARS

The LORD has heard my supplication;
The LORD will receive my prayer.

PSALM 6:9

Read once more the amazing truth in Psalm 6:9. The omnipotent, omnipresent throughout time and space, and totally other God of the universe hears and readily receives your prayers. This infinite God chooses to be involved in your life. Even though the universe cannot contain Him in His vastness, He tenderly bends down to take your hand and listen to your supplications. In the personal relationship we have with the Lord God, He shares His strength and His wisdom with us. When we are weary or faint, He bears us up. We can trust Him in every circumstance and be confident that His Spirit will guide us through life's valleys. The Bible describes our listening God as all powerful yet loving, a God who cares deeply for every human being He created. Yes, He cares deeply for you.

The words of Psalm 17:6–8 beautifully convey the psalmist's awareness that God truly cares and is sensitive to the needs of His people:

> *I have called upon You, for You will hear me, O God;*
> *Incline Your ear to me, and hear my speech.*
> *Show Your marvelous lovingkindness by Your right hand,*
> *O You who save those who trust in You*
> *From those who rise up against them.*
> *Keep me as the apple of Your eye;*
> *Hide me under the shadow of Your wings.*

Clearly, Old Testament believers knew that God hears the prayers of His people and cares about us. The psalmist confidently proclaimed, "The righteous cry out, and the LORD hears, and delivers them out of all their troubles" (Psalm 34:17). So never hesitate to cry out to your God who does receive His people's prayers. He will bless you as, by praying, you act in trust and trust Him to act.

Blessed is he whose transgression is forgiven,
  Whose sin is covered.
Blessed is the man to whom the LORD does not
  impute iniquity,
And in whose spirit there is no deceit.

PSALM 32:1–2

SPECIFIC PRAYERS

—⁕—

FORGIVENESS

The Grace of Forgiveness

In Him we have redemption through His blood, the forgiveness of sins, according to the riches of His grace which He made to abound toward us in all wisdom and prudence, having made known to us the mystery of His will, according to His good pleasure which He purposed in Himself.

Ephesians 1:7–9

Gracious Lord Jesus, because You shed Your blood and died on the cross for me, God has forgiven every sin I have committed, and I "have redemption through [Your] blood, the forgiveness of sins." The words *thank You* are woefully inadequate. By God's grace and according to His eternal plan, my choice to put my faith in You as my Savior and Lord has given me the freedom from punishment for my sins. Instead, by divine grace, I am able to live each day guided by the Spirit and in Your loving presence. Yours is amazing grace indeed.

No Condemnation

There is . . . no condemnation to those who are in Christ Jesus,
who do not walk according to the flesh, but according to the Spirit.
For the law of the Spirit of life in Christ Jesus has made me free
from the law of sin and death.

ROMANS 8:1–2

Just and merciful God, Your Word declares that "there is . . . no condemnation to those who are in Christ Jesus" when we who name Him "Savior" and "Lord" walk "according to [Your] Spirit." I am blessed to be one of those people, good and merciful God. You have "made me free from the law of sin and death" by crediting Your Son's death to my account. I am awed and humbled by Your immeasurable grace and sacrificial love.

....

....

....

....

....

....

....

....

DARKNESS AND LIGHT

*Walk worthy of the Lord . . . giving thanks to the Father who
has qualified us to be partakers of the inheritance of the saints
in the light. He has delivered us from the power of darkness and
conveyed us into the kingdom of the Son of His love, in whom we
have redemption through His blood, the forgiveness of sins.*

COLOSSIANS 1:10, 12–14

All-powerful God, You have "delivered [me] from the power of darkness." What a blessing to now live in the light of Jesus Christ—the light of truth, love, and hope. Thank You, Father, for accepting me into Your family on the basis of Your Son's ultimate sacrifice. Jesus' shed blood means for me "redemption . . . the forgiveness of sins." I say, "Thank You," but may I say that with my life as well: enable me to, out of gratitude for forgiveness and salvation, "walk worthy of the Lord."

THE BLESSING OF FORGIVENESS

Bless the LORD, O my soul, . . .
Who forgives all your iniquities, . . .
Who redeems your life from destruction,
Who crowns you with lovingkindness and tender mercies, . . .
So that your youth is renewed like the eagle's. . . .
As far as the east is from the west,
So far has He removed our transgressions from us.

PSALM 103:2–5, 12

I join with David, great and gracious Lord, in praising You! You bless me each day with Your lovingkindness. You forgive me when I fail You, and You do so time after time after time. And You remove those sins "as far as the east is from the west." You have—as David proclaimed—forgiven my iniquities, healed my diseases, and redeemed my life from destruction. And You didn't stop there. You bless me with "lovingkindness and tender mercies." As if that weren't enough, I do ask that You would strengthen me so that I may joyfully and effectively tell others of Your saving grace and the blessing of Your forgiveness.

....

....

....

....

GOD IS GRACIOUS

"I, even I, am He who blots out your transgressions for My own sake;
And I will not remember your sins."

What an amazing promise! What a gracious God! You blot "out [my] transgressions for [Your] own sake; and [You] will not remember [my] sins." Sweeter words have never been spoken! No better gift has ever been given! May I share this sweet and life-giving truth with those You put in my path who have yet to hear it! And please help me, I pray, to be mindful that you are with me in all circumstances, for You are the giver and taker of all things.

SPECIFIC PRAYERS

— ⁘ —

GOD'S PROMISES

OUR UNCHANGING GOD

"For I am the LORD, I do not change;
Therefore you are not consumed, O sons of Jacob.
Yet from the days of your fathers
You have gone away from My ordinances
And have not kept them.
Return to Me, and I will return to you,"
Says the LORD of hosts.

MALACHI 3:6–7

In this world characterized by busyness, hurriedness, and change, I am thankful, Lord God, that You "do not change." Your character—Your patience, grace, mercy, love—will never change. And You will never withdraw Your invitation for me to confess my sins and receive Your forgiveness. When I stray—when I "have gone away from [Your] ordinances and have not kept them"—You will honor my sincere repentance and receive me back into Your fold. Thank You, unchanging God, for Your everlasting love. Strengthen my commitment to live in Your presence and for Your purpose that I may serve You faithfully.

WAIT ON THE LORD

*The everlasting God, the L*ORD*,*
The Creator of the ends of the earth,
Neither faints nor is weary.
His understanding is unsearchable.
He gives power to the weak, . . .
*But those who wait on the L*ORD
Shall renew their strength;
They shall mount up with wings like eagles,
They shall run and not be weary,
They shall walk and not faint.

ISAIAH 40:28–29, 31

L ord Jesus, You walked this earth, and You know human weariness. So You know what a wonderful promise this is: "Those who wait on the LORD shall renew their strength." You never faint or feel weary. Yet I, made of dust, can find myself low on strength. But I am energized just reading once again that You will enable me to "mount up with wings like eagles." Lord, with the renewed strength You give me, may I continue to praise You, to trust You, to follow You, to serve You—all for Your glory!

....

....

....

....

....

DO NOT WORRY

"Do not worry about your life, what you will eat or what you will drink; nor about your body, what you will put on. Is not life more than food and the body more than clothing? Look at the birds of the air, for they neither sow nor reap nor gather into barns; yet your heavenly Father feeds them. Are you not of more value than they?"

MATTHEW 6:25–26

Father God, thank You for taking care of me. You know my needs and provide for them, You understand that I worry and reassure me not to. Every time I notice "the birds of the air"—made by Your hand and fed by Your hand—may I be encouraged to trust You more. And then in trust may I generously share all that You give me and freely speak of You, my faithful Provider.

....

....

....

....

....

....

....

Rest for Your Soul

"Come to Me, all you who labor and are heavy laden, and I will give you rest. Take My yoke upon you and learn from Me, for I am gentle and lowly in heart, and you will find rest for your souls. For My yoke is easy and My burden is light."

MATTHEW 11:28–30

My Shepherd and my Lord, I thank You for this invitation. Thank You for being "gentle and lowly in heart." And thank You that, when I come to You with an open heart, I "will find rest for [my soul]." Refresh my empty heart and weary soul that I might receive the joy of Your presence. You have taught me that "[Your] yoke is easy and [Your] burden is light." Lord, I trust You and I receive that promise. Let Your light reflect through me so that others will see the power of Your Spirit and live to glorify You.

Delight in God's Law

Blessed is the man
Who walks not in the counsel of the ungodly,
Nor stands in the path of sinners,
Nor sits in the seat of the scornful;
But his delight is in the law of the LORD,
And in His law he meditates day and night.
He shall be like a tree
Planted by the rivers of water,
That brings forth its fruit in its season,
Whose leaf also shall not wither;
And whatever he does shall prosper.

PSALM 1:1–3

Holy God, this sinner definitely needs Your guidance as I walk through this life, so I thank You for the counsel I can find in "the law of the LORD." Please give me, I pray, a thirst to know better the counsel of Your Word, to meditate on it, and to obey it. I also ask that You transform my heart that I might truly delight in Your Word. Bring forth the fruit which comes from living close to You, and bless me, Lord, that I may bless others with the living testimony of Your love and provision.

....

....

....

....

THE FEAR OF THE LORD

The fear of the LORD leads to life,
And he who has it will abide in satisfaction;
He will not be visited with evil.

PROVERBS 19:23

Fear of the Lord—I see that phrase throughout Your Word, often rephrased as a command to Your people. I want to obey, Lord: I want to show You the respect You deserve, and I want to live in light of the truth that You are God, You are in control of all things. And when I don't understand the trials You've allowed in my life, may I "abide in satisfaction," knowing contentment because I know You and I am choosing to trust You. Thank You for Your promise to protect me from evil and thank You that living in "the fear of the Lord" means living life as You designed it to be lived.

....

....

....

....

....

....

....

....

GOD'S PRIORITIES

The kingdom of God is not eating and drinking, but righteousness and peace and joy in the Holy Spirit. For he who serves Christ in these things is acceptable to God and approved by men.

ROMANS 14:17–18

Wise and holy Lord, I do find it hard to live according to Your priorities. I understand that pursuing what the world deems important will not lead to a God-pleasing or satisfying life. What You value is a life characterized by "righteousness and peace and joy in the Holy Spirit." As I walk with You and serve You, may I know the presence of Your Spirit and the righteousness, peace, and joy He brings.

....

....

....

....

....

....

....

....

He Will Deliver Us

Shadrach, Meshach, and Abed-Nego answered and said to the king . . .
"Our God whom we serve is able to deliver us from the burning fiery
furnace, and He will deliver us from your hand, O king. But if not, let
it be known to you, O king, that we do not serve your gods, nor will we
worship the gold image which you have set up."

Daniel 3:16–18

Almighty God, by Your grace, I have yet to risk my life because of my faith in Your Son. But Nebuchadnezzar was ready to throw Your followers into a blazing furnace for not bowing down and worshipping a statue of the king, yet these three men were not going to back down. Theirs is the kind of faith I want to have. May I speak with confidence: "[My] God whom [I] serve is able to deliver [me]." Then, whatever happens, may I remain loyal to You. Lord, I want to be faithful to You no matter what happens in my life. Thank You for the protection and strength You promise to give me even as You gave Shadrach, Meshach, and Abed-Nego.

THE LIGHT OF THE WORLD

"You are the light of the world. A city that is set on a hill cannot be hidden. Nor do they light a lamp and put it under a basket, but on a lampstand, and it gives light to all who are in the house. Let your light so shine before men, that they may see your good works and glorify your Father in heaven."

MATTHEW 5:14–16

Lord Jesus, two thousand years ago you stated to Your people, "You are the light of the world." And, today, this dark world still needs Your people to be Your light—to shine Your hope and truth into their lostness, emptiness, and despair. I am humbled by this honor and responsibility. May I always walk so closely to You and be so filled with Your Spirit that Your light shines brightly through me to everyone around me. And when I am asked about that light, please enable me to clearly set forth the reason for the hope that is in me.

....

....

....

....

....

....

....

TRUST, DELIGHT, AND COMMIT

Trust in the LORD, and do good;
Dwell in the land, and feed on His faithfulness.
Delight yourself also in the LORD,
And He shall give you the desires of your heart.
Commit your way to the LORD,
Trust also in Him,
And He shall bring it to pass.

PSALM 37:3–5

W ise and wonderful God, You are very clear about the kind of life that pleases You. In the verses above You call Your people to "trust in the LORD . . . Delight yourself also in the LORD . . . Commit your way to the LORD." You alone can know my heart and how well I'm trusting, how much I'm delighting, and how strong I'm committing; however, those around me will be able to know if I am obeying Your command to "do good." Please direct my steps so that I do the good that You would have me do—and may You be glorified.

....

....

....

....

....

Communion with God

"I am the vine, you are the branches. He who abides in Me, and I in him, bears much fruit; for without Me you can do nothing. If anyone does not abide in Me, he is cast out as a branch and is withered; and they gather them and throw them into the fire, and they are burned. If you abide in Me, and My words abide in you, you will ask what you desire, and it shall be done for you. By this My Father is glorified, that you bear much fruit; so you will be My disciples."

JOHN 15:5–8

The only way we can play a significant role in the kingdom of God is to allow Jesus to live in us and work through us. Apart from Him, we can do nothing. In Him, we can do anything He calls us to do. That is why the life of a believer is to be an abiding life: we are to walk closely with God every moment of every day. We are to stay in unbroken communion with our heavenly Father.

How can we do that, though, when each one of us is busy with life's responsibilities and demands? We do so by choosing to do so! We must decide to set aside a time to abide—to pray, to read God's Word, to be alone with Jesus. God longs for us to enjoy a rich and intimate relationship, unbroken fellowship, and transformative communion with Him. Only then will we grow in holiness; only then will we bear fruit.

SPECIFIC PRAYERS

— ❧ · ❧ —

PRAYERS

FOR

ETERNAL LIFE

THE GIFT OF ETERNAL LIFE

This is the testimony: that God has given us eternal life, and this life is in His Son. He who has the Son has life; he who does not have the Son of God does not have life. These things I have written to you who believe in the name of the Son of God, that you may know that you have eternal life, and that you may continue to believe in the name of the Son of God.

1 JOHN 5:11–13

Almighty and eternal God, You created us to live forever—either with You or apart from You. The choice is ours. As one who has named Your Son "Savior" and "Lord," I praise You for the gift of eternal life with You and for the purpose and the hope for this life embedded in that reality.

When life's difficulties bring loss, hurt, and sadness, the promise of eternal life with You gives me hope. I can look forward to a time and a place where there will be no more crying or pain. I thank You, Lord, for the gift of eternal life with You.

....

....

....

....

....

....

LET TRUTH ABIDE IN YOU

Therefore let that abide in you which you heard from the beginning. If what you heard from the beginning abides in you, you also will abide in the Son and in the Father. And this is the promise that He has promised us—eternal life.

1 JOHN 2:24–25

Almighty God, my Rock and my Fortress, whatever the winds of this world's popular opinion, help me never let go of Your life-giving, life-saving gospel. In the words of the apostle John, "let that [truth about Jesus Christ] abide in [me]," that I may stand strong as Your light to encourage fellow believers and to attract nonbelievers to Your saving grace. I yearn to tell others of Your saving grace, for You, Lord, are the joy of my life and the hope of my heart. And You alone offer an eternal life of joy.

THE WAY, THE TRUTH, AND THE LIFE

*Jesus said to [Thomas], "I am the way, the truth, and the life. No
one comes to the Father except through Me. If you had known
Me, you would have known My Father also; and from now on you
know Him and have seen Him."*

JOHN 14:6–7

Lord Jesus, You are "the way, the truth, and the life," and
no one can come into the presence of our holy God except
through You, through the forgiveness that Your perfect sacrifice on the cross made possible. You are the Christ, the sinless Son of
God, whose shed blood cleanses me from all unrighteousness. My desire
is to live for You day and night and to spend every moment in Your presence. Help me to know You in such a way that we will walk together
through time and eternity.

SPECIFIC PRAYERS

—❧⸱❧—

SALVATION

SET FREE FROM SIN

Having been set free from sin, and having become slaves of God, you have your fruit to holiness, and the end, everlasting life. For the wages of sin is death, but the gift of God is eternal life in Christ Jesus our Lord.

ROMANS 6:22–23

Great is Your mercy, Lord God! Great is Your grace! Thanks to You, I have "been set free from sin"! Thanks to You, I realize what an oppressive master sin is. What a joy and blessing to now be a "[slave] of God." Thank You, Father, that following Your commands and living in Your light will mean greater freedom than life apart from You can ever offer. What an infinitely precious gift of salvation You offer me in Jesus. Place within my heart the fruit of Your holiness that my life might reflect the light of Your glory. Help me to live in the power of Your unchanging Word and declare Your great works to a lost world.

Having Life More Abundantly

"I am the door. If anyone enters by Me, he will be saved, and will go in and out and find pasture. The thief does not come except to steal, and to kill, and to destroy. I have come that they may have life, and that they may have it more abundantly."

John 10:9–10

Lord of love and Lord of life, Your Word is clear: You are the one Door to the Father and to the abundant life available only in Him. How wonderful to know and to live in that truth! You gave Your life for me that I might be saved from the consequences of my sin, delivered from an eternity apart from God. You gave Your life for me that I might know life "more abundantly" by living it—now and forever—in relationship with the One who created me, the One who designed my life. I praise You for Your saving grace.

THE BREAD OF LIFE

"Most assuredly, I say to you, he who believes in Me has everlasting life. I am the bread of life."

JOHN 6:47–48

Lord Jesus, Bread of Life, Your descriptions of Yourself are rich with meaning. Bread is a staple, a basic element, a necessary food. Yet I can too easily treat my relationship with You as an extra, an option. And I can too easily take for granted the presence of bread and the nourishment and comfort it provides. Please forgive me when I take Your presence for granted. Help me, Lord, to appreciate Your spiritually nourishing, comforting, and life-sustaining presence.

STAND AT THE DOOR AND KNOCK

"Behold, I stand at the door and knock. If anyone hears My voice and opens the door, I will come in to him and dine with him, and he with Me. To him who overcomes I will grant to sit with Me on My throne, as I also overcame and sat down with My Father on His throne."

REVELATION 3:20–21

Lord Jesus, what a picture of grace! You come to me, You pursue me, and You "stand at the door and knock." You don't force Yourself into my life; You don't pull rank and take over my heart. You knock, and You wait for me to answer. Thank You, Lord, that You came to me. Thank You for enabling me to hear Your voice. And thank You for working in my heart so that I opened the door. I thank You for the gift of salvation and the gift of spending eternity with You.

CONFESS . . . AND BELIEVE

If you confess with your mouth the Lord Jesus and believe in your heart that God has raised Him from the dead, you will be saved. For with the heart one believes unto righteousness, and with the mouth confession is made unto salvation.

ROMANS 10:9–10

Lord Jesus, the steps of salvation—*confess* and *believe*—sound simple enough, yet where those steps take me defies description! You have helped me recognize and confess that I am a sinner, that I have lived far away from You, and that I need a Savior. I have asked and continue to ask Your forgiveness for all the ways I have fallen short of Your standards and disappointed You. You are the Son of God and You gave Yourself up to die on the cross that I might be forgiven and have eternal life. May I never hesitate to confess publicly my faith in You for I can do nothing without You.

SPECIFIC PRAYERS

SERVANTHOOD

Follow Me

*"He who loves his life will lose it, and he who hates his life in
this world will keep it for eternal life. If anyone serves Me, let
him follow Me; and where I am, there My servant will be also. If
anyone serves Me, him My Father will honor."*

John 12:25–26

O heavenly Father, I say that You are my greatest priority in life, but I realize I don't always live out that commitment. My calendar, my daily to-do list, my bank account balance, my use of time—there is much evidence that I love my life and that I too often serve myself. Place within my heart the desire to follow You. You have promised that where You are, Your faithful servant will be. Keep me in the center of Your will and lead me through the guidance of Your Holy Spirit that I will faithfully serve Your purpose and tell others of Your hand on my life. For You, O Lord, are greatly to be praised.

A LIVING SACRIFICE

I beseech you therefore, brethren, by the mercies of God, that you present your bodies a living sacrifice, holy, acceptable to God, which is your reasonable service. And do not be conformed to this world, but be transformed by the renewing of your mind, that you may prove what is that good and acceptable and perfect will of God.

ROMANS 12:1–2

What a high calling—to present my body "a living sacrifice, holy, acceptable to God." That is the position I want to be in so that You can use me for Your kingdom purposes. So help me lay myself on the altar—to submit my heart to You that Your will becomes my desire Lord, make me a willing and obedient servant for the growth of Your kingdom and the celebration of Your glory. By Your power, may I live so that one day I will hear from You, "Well done, My good and faithful servant."

*And we desire that each one of you show
the same diligence to the full assurance of
hope until the end, that you do not become
sluggish, but imitate those who through faith
and patience inherit the promises.*

HEBREWS 6:11–12

SPECIFIC PRAYERS

PATIENCE

Waiting on the Lord

The Lord will wait, that He may be gracious to you;
And therefore He will be exalted, that He may have mercy on you.
For the Lord is a God of justice;
Blessed are all those who wait for Him.

Isaiah 30:18

Lord God, Your Word teaches not only that You are gracious, merciful, and just, but also that I sometimes have to wait for those blessings. You have promised that You "will wait, that [You] may be gracious to [me]." Perhaps You are waiting for me to look to You, to obey You, to submit more fully to Your lordship as I wait for Your blessings to come. Lord, as I wait, please give me the desire to seek and to trust Your perfect timing and will in my life. And please sustain me as I strive to live each moment in Your presence with peace and joy and, yes, patience.

ONE SOURCE OF PATIENCE

*Count it all joy when you fall into various trials, knowing that the
testing of your faith produces patience. But let patience have its
perfect work, that you may be perfect and complete, lacking nothing.*

JAMES 1:2–4

O Lord, I must admit there is nothing joyful in the trials
that I face. Yet I realize that You use trials and suffering for "the testing of [my] faith," testing that "produces
patience." May keeping my eyes on You enable me to "count [trials] all
joy." And, I pray, may "patience [do] its perfect work" in my life, perhaps
the work of growing my trust in You—trust in Your good plans and perfect timing—and the comfort of knowing that I am most blessed when I
walk more closely with You.

WAITING PATIENTLY

I waited patiently for the LORD;
And He inclined to me,
And heard my cry.
He also brought me up out of a horrible pit,
Out of the miry clay,
And set my feet upon a rock,
And established my steps.
He has put a new song in my mouth—
Praise to our God;
Many will see it and fear,
And will trust in the LORD.

PSALM 40:1–3

Creator God, You know that patience does not come easily to me. So I thank You for David's testimony to the value of waiting patiently for You to act. Too often my initial reaction is to try to solve my problems on my own; too often I seek other sources of help before I cry out to You. Grant me the patience and renew my strength to wait for You and Your direction. Then, as David did, may I sing "a new song" of "praise to [my] God," and may You use that song of praise for Your glory.

....

....

....

....

Pathway to Prayer

*"If My people who are called by My name will humble themselves,
and pray and seek My face, and turn from their wicked ways, then I
will hear from heaven, and will forgive their sin and heal their land."*

2 Chronicles 7:14

Prayer is one opportunity God gives us to become intimately acquainted with Him. When we go to Him, humbling ourselves and seeking forgiveness, when we listen for His voice as well as speak from our heart, we build a personal relationship with Him. In prayer we become vulnerable to God and express our dependence on Him, we become transformed by Him, and we are refreshed by His guidance, His peace, and His love. And in prayer we seek God's will instead of our own.

Whenever we talk to the Father, we are to make each request for help and guidance in the name of Jesus. The bottom line of all our prayers is simple: "Thy will be done." So, yes, we pray earnestly and we pray specifically and we pray confidently and we pray with perseverance. And always we pray, "Thy will be done."

All the ways of a man are pure in his own eyes,
  But the Lord weighs the spirits.

Commit your works to the Lord,
  And your thoughts will be established.

PROVERBS 16:2–3

SPECIFIC PRAYERS

—⊱⋅⋅⊰—

SPIRITUAL COMMITMENT

I GIVE YOU MY LIFE

LORD, I hope for Your salvation,
And I do Your commandments.
My soul keeps Your testimonies,
And I love them exceedingly.
I keep Your precepts and Your testimonies,
For all my ways are before You.

PSALM 119:166–168

Lord God, I give You my life; I give You all that I am; and I lay "all my ways . . . before You." Lead me on the path of righteousness so that I might serve You in truth and in spirit. Lord, I want to live out my commitment to You, not just talk about it. I want to serve where You want me to serve, in Your power and for Your glory. Here I am, Lord. Send me.

TO THE VERY END

Your testimonies I have taken as a heritage forever,
For they are the rejoicing of my heart.
I have inclined my heart to perform Your statutes
Forever, to the very end.

PSALM 119:111–112

Eternal and omnipotent God, Your Word—where You set forth "Your testimonies . . . [and] Your statutes"—is my guide for living each day for You. May I find in Your testimonies direction for my life. May I live according to Your statutes in a way that honors You. And as I do so, I ask You to fill me with joy that sustains, so that I may serve You "forever, to the very end" and always for Your glory.

HOLD FAST

Let us draw near with a true heart in full assurance of faith,
having our hearts sprinkled from an evil conscience and our
bodies washed with pure water. Let us hold fast the confession of
our hope without wavering, for He who promised is faithful.

HEBREWS 10:22–23

Almighty God, I can only live out my commitment to You in Your power. So I "draw near [to You] with a true heart in full assurance of faith," in full assurance that You who calls me to a life devoted to You will empower me to live that way. I long to know You completely and to live each moment in Your presence. You call me to "hold fast the confession of [my] hope," and I ask You to hold fast to me each step of the way. For You, O Lord, have promised to be faithful; therefore, help me to be faithful in every way.

....

....

....

....

....

....

....

....

A CLOSING PROMISE

"Because he has set his love upon Me, therefore I will deliver him;
I will set him on high, because he has known My name.
He shall call upon Me, and I will answer him;
I will be with him in trouble;
I will deliver him and honor him.
With long life I will satisfy him,
And show him My salvation."

PSALM 91:14–16

How blessed we are that God listens attentively to our prayers. How blessed we are to be able to come before Him with our confessions, thanksgiving, praise, supplication, and intercession. According to His promises, when we place our love and our trust in Him—and our prayers are evidence of our doing that—we can call upon Him and He "will answer."

And how blessed we are that we can approach the Creator of the universe, the King above all kings, the Author of history, and talk to Him just as directly and transparently, without pretense or hesitation, as we would talk to a beloved friend. Such prayerful communion with God is vital to our spiritual life. Nothing reveals more about us and what we value than the time we spend with our heavenly Father in earnest prayer. So many of the duties of life push aside our quiet times with God; our busyness crowds out the communication with our Lord that we so desperately need.

May we seize every opportunity to spend time with the One who loves us with an everlasting love. When we talk to God and share our deepest thoughts, emotions, and desires, and allow His Spirit to speak to our hearts, we will find ourselves richly blessed.

May your time with God in prayer be a life-giving priority as you walk through each day with your risen Savior, bringing all Glory to Him!

PRAYERS

PRAYERS

PRAYERS

PRAYERS